A KILLER NAMED HATCH
MASSACRE ON POTATO HILL

A True Story

Thomas Blanchfield

authorHOUSE®

AuthorHouse™
1663 Liberty Drive
Bloomington, IN 47403
www.authorhouse.com
Phone: 1-800-839-8640

First published by AuthorHouse 8/24/2009

ISBN: 978-1-4389-9557-1 (sc)

Printed in the United States of America
Bloomington, Indiana

This book is printed on acid-free paper.

This book is dedicated to the New York State Police whose mission is, to serve and defend the People while preserving the rights and dignity Of all.

THE TELL TALE HEART

I think it was his eyes! Yes, it was this! He had the eye of a vulture-a pale blue eye, with a film over it. Whenever it fell upon me, my blood ran cold.

Edgar Allen Poe   1843

Contents

PROLOGUE

There was nothing ordinary about the 365 days in 1973. The memorable names that were headlined were: Nolan Ryan, Bobby Seale, Ken Norton, Spiro Agnew. The news featured: Wounded Knee, Watergate, Boston Celtics and microwave ovens. Cadillac's sold for under $8,000, the minimum salary for major league ballplayers was $15,000. The Viet Nam war came to an end and the crime rate was down 3%.

President Nixon resigned after accepting responsibility for the Watergate break-in, Hank Aaron was within one home run of breaking Babe Ruth's record of 713. The popular novel was "Winds of War," Paul 1V was the Pope, the oil embargo caused Governor Rockefeller to reduce the speed limit to 50 on the Thruway and the best picture of the year was, "The Godfather."

The Town of Steuben was nestled quietly in the center of the State of New York and remained calm and peaceful until the New York State Police set up a command post in the town garage, enlisted the help of U-2's, helicopters and a Military Police Battalion to scour the remote, wooded terrain, looking for bodies. It was unsettling for the locals, usually proud of the community named after Baron Von Steuben, a trained Prussian staff officer, requesting his military expertise to assist our country in the Revolutionary War.

Few enjoyed the excitement, others felt violated and invaded. Potato Hill would be forever referred to as "Murder Mountain." Before the year ended three bodies would be discovered in shallow graves and a neighbor would be arrested for murder. The landscape changed forever.

This is a true crime story, concluded by a guilty verdict that followed the longest and most expensive trial in the 200 year history of Oneida County. During the four months of trial, 260 prosecution exhibits, 125 defense exhibits, 69 witnesses for the prosecution, 17 for the defense and 8,000 pages of testimony would be presented. The verdict of 25 years to life would be imposed on Bernard Paul Hatch on April 11, 1975. Including the jury cost, the county spent over one million dollars.

In anticipation of the length of the trial, it became necessary to call 600 prospective jurors before 16 were selected after the Voir Dire, twelve plus four alternates. It was a difficult commitment and sacrifice. The paradox was that the jury returned a verdict after only nine hours and nineteen minutes of deliberation

Seven years after the sentencing and eighteen years before Hatch would be eligible for parole after serving the minimum, four people met just before Christmas in 1982 to outline a strategy to have published a strong and documented reason to keep Hatch in prison for his natural life and denied parole. There were two direct actors and two who could be described as spectators. The pair who were closest to the investigation and trial were: the prosecutor, Ted Wolff and Zone Sergeant Maynard Roman, New York State Police. The onlookers were Gil Smith, retired Editor of the Utica Observer Dispatch who directed the coverage of the hunt and the trial and the writer, Thomas Blanchfield Criminal Justice Professor. Wolff gathered boxes of records from his office, Roman brought his notes, Smith joined with his reporters pad and Blanchfield contributed with a tape recorder. After informal discussions about our vision and focus, the mission began.

We agreed on our game plan: amass the investigation and trial data, produce a time line, agree on a strategy and produce a manuscript. Royalties and contracts were never alluded to. The primary and sole outcome was unanimous-keep Hatch in prison, Within six weeks, Gil had completed, with adeptness, an introduction and two chapters.

Following the publishers protocol, we forwarded 47 manuscripts, included the required self addressed stamped envelopes (S.A.S E.) gleaning the names and addresses from the Writers Manual and awaited responses. The answers dribbled in, one or two a day, starting in the last week in January, 1983. Within 3 months we received the last declination, all polite but discouraging.

The letters were standard denials including: "We are restricting new acquisitions----although the project has considerable merit----we do wish you luck in placing the manuscript elsewhere----we regret we must decline as it does not fit our publishing programs ----this decision in no way reflects on the quality of the material." The final paragraph, with unanimity, included best wishes for success and they were grateful for our interest. We all agreed that we suffered from a sense of false optimism.

We decided to heed the advice of some of the companies by tapping the literary agents for intercession. Their short reaction was, "It has provincial and not global appeal." Somewhat daunted but not disengaged we forged ahead, interviewing parole and probation officers, psychiatrists, fellow inmates of Hatch, the defense attorney, jurors, the presiding judge, troopers, investigators, pathologists and witnesses. Within two years our aspirations became dormant.

Ted Wolff died in 1984 from lymphatic cancer, Sergeant Roman was found dead in his home on December 9, 1997. Gil Smith suffered as an Alzheimer's patient and passed away in 2002. I received the responsibility to attempt another try as the sole survivor of the quartet.

As our team became decimated through sickness and death, I became tormented by the lack of completion and closure for our assignment. I became haunted by the admonition of Ted and Maynard , "We've got to keep him in prison and off the streets"

Since his first parole eligibility date, 10/15/98, Hatch has been denied release every two years. His next earliest release date is 8/28/10. The date of this writing is December 12, 2008 which gives me a window of twenty months to either forward to the parole board a book, complete with his profile and history, or a 2 page letter summarizing my adamant and forceful stand, not to release him . I have forwarded a similar letter every two years without an acknowledgment, but hopefully it has supported their denials.

My solo expedition to complete the book has not been as simple as I anticipated. I have an overwhelming amount of garnered information, over 300 pages of the NYSP investigation, transcripts of testimony, Ted Wolff's written notes, photographs, reports and voluminous notes from our interviews. My only solace is that my efforts will memorialize the dedication and the passion for justice embraced by Ted, Maynard and Gil.

When the book on Hatch began it didn't need to be composed, it had already been constructed. The writer is not a journalist but someone who inherited the role as author by deaths and default. The years spent in the shadows of law enforcement and never a direct participant, allowed me to be a person from academia who learned more from my students than I could ever teach them. The role of author is unearned but considered a bequest. Arriving at an interview with a yellow, lined pad and a tape recorder, they were my only weapons. My diligence in protecting names of some of the victims, witnesses and descendants of the victims has been paramount. The fear of resurrecting unpleasant memories in families has been plaguing. The exclusive goal is to ensure those who are fearful of the perpetrator's release is that he will never be permitted to assassinate any innocent targets..

The epilogue chosen, "Afterword" was devised after reading Junger's book titled, ":The Perfect Storm." Much of the Hatch story included a variety of information that couldn't be matched with a chapter. It was decided that the miscellaneous data would be best categorized as an "Afterword." The dialogue used was as a result of formal interviews, direct quotes from state troopers, the prosecutor, the appeal ADA, neighbors living in Steuben,, family members, parole, probation and corrections personnel. Words were not altered for grammar or clarity. If a reader discovers errors or inconsistencies, they were done without malice or intent.

Time Line

1905
March 23: DOB Florence (nee Erickson) Hatch, mother, Bernard
July 12: DOB Paul Revere Hatch, father, Bernard

1916
September 18: DOB Mary Rose (nee Byrnes) Turner

1917
August 31: DOB William Turner, divorced husband, Mary Rose

1919-1923
Paul Revere Hatch, U.S. Army

1936
Marriage, Paul Hatch, Florence Erickson

1940
March 5: DOB Bernard Paul Hatch

1943
August 2: Baptism, Bernard Hatch

1945
December 1: DOB Victoria, sister of Bernard

1946
Hatch family moved from Goshen N.Y. to Remsen N.Y.

1947
November 27: DOB Linda (nee Aiken) Cady

1949
June 19: DOB Clyde Turner, son of Mary Rose

1951
September: Hatch enrolled in Deansboro Central
October: Hatch hospitalized, 4 months, tractor rollover

1952
January 14: Death, Paul Revere Hatch

1956
May: Hatch quits high school

1958
September 6: Hatch meets Andrea (nee Rooney) State Fair

1959
July 25: Marriage, Hatch and Andrea, Staten Island, N.Y.
October 8: Hatch enlists in U.S.M.C.

1960
February 22: DOB Cassandra

1961
February 4: Hatch reconciles with wife, sees Cassandra for first time

1962
September 28: death, Patrick Rooney, father of Andrea

1963
October 22: Arrest of Hatch, kidnapping, rape and firearms

1964
August 3: conviction, Hatch sentenced 25 to life

1965
January 11: Hatch, dishonorable discharge, U.S.M.C

1966
February 16: Reverse and modification by Appellate Division
August 22, DOB Lisa Ann Cady

1969
August 4: Hatch paroled from Attica Correctional Facility

1970
January 30: Linda Cady in love with Hatch (diary and letter)
February 25, Cady letter to Lopez, "In love with Hatch"
March 10: DOB Marc Smith, son of Andrea
April 14: Lorraine Zinicola moves to Utica from Hartford CT
Late April: Hatch gives diamond ring to Linda Cady
June 19: Note from Linda Cady to mother, moving to Syracuse, withdraws $345.00 from savings account
June 20: Linda and Lisa Ann Cady sighted at Soule Road, last seen
June 2:, scratches on Hatch's left cheek and jaw, observed by fellow employee
July 2: Linda and Lisa Cady reported missing, U.P.D.
October 21: Hatch under parole supervision
November 18: Hatch and Lorraine Zinicola dating

1971
January 11: Lorraine Zinicola separated from husband, moved from mother's home
June 3: Note from Lorraine Zinicola to mother, "Going south with sons"
July 8: Zinicola and sons last seen
July 9: Zinicola withdraws $4,000.00 from Cornhill Savings and Loan, $2,000.00 in cash, $2,000.00 in Certified check cashed in Amsterdam, N.Y.
September 8: Missing persons report filed U.P.D. by Ms. Penar, Joseph 7, James 4, Mark 2, missing since July 8
December 23: DWI arrest, Hatch

1972
January 12: Joanne Pecheone murdered and raped

March 9: Hatch arrested for rape first and remanded to jail

December:16: Hatch trial, found not guilty, remanded for parole violation

1973

April 18: Mary Rose Turner has haircut at Utica School of Beauty Culture

April 21: Mrs. Turner drives to Albany, stays one hour in motel

April 23: Mrs. Turner has accident on Thruway

April 24: Mrs. Turner has shampoo and hair set, Utica School of Beauty Culture

April 25: Mrs. Turner calls in sick to work

April 26: Mrs. Turner last seen alive on Court Street at 3-3:30 a.m. Hatch leaves work at 7:00 a.m. observed in Steuben by 6 witnesses at 4 locations between 10-12 noon. Trooper Chaffee responds to Weaver's call, retrieves evidence in early evening

April 27: Trooper Broccoli delivers evidence to Lab. Hatch calls in sick. Daughter said he was vomiting

April 28: Hatch drives to Holland Patent, has 2 tires removed and 2 replaced

April 29: Body unearthed from shallow grave, identified at morgue by brother and son of Mary Rose Turner

May 1: Bohling Shell burglarized, time sheets missing for 4/27

May 2: Search warrant executed at trailer occupied by Hatch. Cars impounded. Clothing discovered and identified by Mrs. Aiken as being owned by Linda and Lisa Ann Cady

May 4: Hand discovered identified as Mrs. Turner's

May 6: Three toys found on the bank of Tannery Creek: Shell Oil Truck, red fir engine and blue Jeepster

October 17: Hatch indicted by Grand Jury, arrested and held without bail

October 20: Hatch parole expiration date

December 8: Hunters discovers skull and body parts, Latteiman Road, Steuben

December 11: Remains identified by archeologist and coroner as Linda and Lisa Cady

December 18: Burned clothing found near Turner grave identified as belonging to Zinicola and three sons. Christine Chapple moves to Nebraska

1974
April 27: Andrea, divorced wife of Hatch, commits suicide after visiting ex-husband in jail
November 6: Trial begins in Rome

1975
March 3: Trial ends
March 6: Jury returns verdict of guilty, murder 2d degree
April 2: Hatch slashes wrist in jail
April 11: Hatch sentenced to 25 to life

1983
February 23: Appeal by defendant argued in Rochester, unanimous decision-denied

1994
May 13: Edward A. Wolff, Jr. died

1997
December 9: Maynard T Roman died

2000
March 5: Judge John J. Walsh died

2002
Gil Smith died

Chapter 1

THE MESSENGER

"Shoot the messenger" is a passage that describes, metaphorically, a blameless person who brings bad news. James Weaver didn't care if the state police thought of him as an accused, he knew what he saw.

Mr. James Weaver was stout but a healthy stout, citizen. At 265 pounds and an inch or two over 6 feet, he described himself proudly as "Powerful." It was questionable as to whether he had a set of upper teeth. His daily uniform was: white socks, black boots, bib overalls and a blue T shirt beneath a long sleeved plaid shirt. He was a dedicated farmer.

Whether in the house, the barn or the fields he'd wear a baseball cap, tilted a bit left of center. He was proud of his routine when he voiced, "I never wear a watch and I never miss a noon meal. I walk in the back door at the stroke of twelve, seven days a week." His biological clock was always accurate.

He was his own best audience, enjoying his provincial sense of humor and didn't wait for a reaction from the listener. He thought of himself as comical and he was that. The New York State Police wouldn't share his self portrayal. His observations were precise, candid, without flourish, that would become invaluable when he testified about the events of April 26, 1973.

Described by his neighbors as "A character but a little scary at times" would be accurate. Raised on a farm in Steuben, one of nine children, six boys, three girls, he was a typical homesteader. You felt a sense of survival as he reviewed the harsh winters in upstate New York as a youth. The calloused hands showed a life of manual labor and

1

living off the land. He didn't blame himself for his limited education or his unpolished speech.

He volunteered the reason for his limited schooling as he said, "We were snowed in from early December to mid March every year. The roads didn't get plowed and we just existed for the winter, just like the bears and the raccoons. That's why I never got a "high education." He didn't complain nor apologize about his plight, it was a simple fact.

Appraising his family Weaver said, "Elton is the eldest, still lives with Ma up on the family farm." He shifts his mood as he continues speaking of Elton and became uncharacteristically gentle and empathetic as he said, "Elton was nervous, ya know, nervous all his life, still nervous today. Ma takes good care of him. He was the only one out of the nine of us like that." He tugged at his cap and looked away as he described his brother. He sped through the birth order: Everett, Viola, Sophie and suddenly stopped, grabbed his cap again and didn't continue.

James sent a sensitive signal as he spoke of those who had a "high education." He also had an undisguised problem with authority as he jumped to his military career. He had disdain for the Army, but also a sense of gratitude about what they taught him. James was a draftee and was called to the Induction Center in Syracuse, N.Y. for a physical. He was summoned to a building on the southwest corner of South Salinas Street named the Chimes Building. Weaver decided to call it the "Charms Building." He continued, "In '59, they kept callin' me to report to the Charms Building, so I went. Stood around all day, bare-ass, with a bunch of guys I didn't know. That ain't my idea of fun. Never asked for a farm deferment, hell, with eight other kids, includin' Elton, to milk fifteen head, that ain't nothin'. They wouldn't need me on the farm anyway. Wait 'till you hear this-they told me to piss in a bottle and if I couldn't, get someone else to. I told them to take me in the Army and they did. Now ain't that some shit?"

His intransigence grew as he discussed his correspondence with the Commander in Chief, Dwight Eisenhower. His notice from the Selective Service Board read, "Greetings" and signed by the president. He showed a degree of tacit acceptance as he continued, "Hell, I never met the son-of-bitch and he's sayin' to me, greetins'. So, I end up at Brooke Army Hospital in Texas for awhile and never been south of Madison, New York. Finished at Brooke and they put me on a train and ship me to Walter Reed in Washington. Now I'm close to my pal Dwight but never got to see him and never say ' greetins.' They gave me a lot of terms to learn and I kept tellin' them that I didn't have a high education, so they were slow about it and so was I. That's when I learned all those body parts, words like testines and inwards and a whole lot of other shit. Saw a bunch of them, you know."

His recalcitrant tour as a medic would tend to reinforce his scrutiny of April 26, 1973. Weaver would become the leadoff witness for the prosecution, despite his poor attendance in the winter and his limited education. He served his country reluctantly but he didn't recriminate about being under-educated, the military seemed to complement what he missed.

Weaver's farmhouse was atypical, unpainted, 70 years old, no curtains on any of the windows. The average person driving by would assume it was vacant. He rose with the sun, went to bed when it set. Farmers have an instinct for the chores that need to be cared for. Their bodies tell them when they are tired and when they are hungry.

One of his chores slated was cutting brush with a borrowed tractor in a field south of his home and barn. He knew that it was between 9 and 9:30 a.m. when he saw something on Potato Hill Road traveling north. It was late in April and the growing season was soon to arrive. It had been a heavy winter in upstate with 110 inches of snow falling in the past 5 months. James placed himself at between 500 and 800 feet from the road when he saw something odd. When the defense attorney grilled him on the witness stand 19 months later and asked, "Why were you there Mr. Weaver?" his reply was to the point, " Didn't get to do it in the fall!"

He was pretty close to being on schedule, finish by noon and walk in the back door for dinner as his biological clock ordered. He had to dismount from the tractor on occasion in order to clear the boulders that the frost had heaved during the winter. He was positioned to see clearly, with no obstructions, Potato Hill Road. The four foot stone fence didn't hinder his view. He could clearly see the crown in the road as he watched his flanks so he wouldn't damage the tractor's blade. He heard a car going north and looked toward the road, then wiped his eyes for a better look.

As the car passed his vision he noticed something being dragged behind it, about eight feet from the rear bumper. He said it was white. His instinct told him that it might be a cow. His second thought was that it might be a wedding cortege, possibly cans inside a sheet tied to the bumper. He later conceded that it was six, not eight feet behind the bumper.

Completing his cutting, his afternoon schedule included a trip to Boonville, twenty minutes away, and fill the two ten gallon cans of gasoline. The replenishment was protocol when you borrowed a piece of equipment, return it with a full tank even if it was half full when you picked it up. He went directly to the general store named Agway. It was a "Soup to nuts" place to shop and a farmers delight. You could buy chicken wire, refrigerators, hardware, rabbit food or flea collars, all in one stop. It was Weaver's favorite. James had a resistance to change and referenced it by the former name, GLF. He also called his couch a settee.

He relished his trips to town, visit a bit, often stop at the local diner for a piece of homemade pie. As he passed his neighbors farms he felt cavalier since he could tell that they weren't dong as well as he was, based on the upkeep and equipment.

Arriving at Agway, he immediately began a dialogue with the help. They knew James too well, predictable and humorous. James opened with his tirade about the oil shortage, the price of gasoline and in his words, " I blame those f-----g A-a-a-rabs", as he called anyone from the Mid East.

Floyd was a clerk and a long term employee, even when it was GLF. He enjoyed playing the straight man and knew the answer, when he asked, "How's the old lady Jim? " "Still cranky, still an attendant, but not to me." He was proud of his mate's employment at the Psychiatric Center, and, as he called it, "The funny farm." Floyd cackled as if it was the first time he heard it. Weaver then took a serious turn as he moved close to a barrel of seed and shared his impression of the car dragging earlier, "Saw somethin' wacky today and don't know what to make of it." Knowing he was in for a long harangue, Floyd leaned on the barrel. Another clerk joined them, Elmer, and listened to Jim's explanation.

"What I saw was something bein' lugged behind this car, maybe a pig, not big enough to be a cow as I first figured." The words were vague and without a premise, they didn't offer a sound conclusion. "They may have been part of a weddin', you know how kids today drag shit behind their cars and such. They weren't blowin' their horns though."

Their attention was diverted when a customer had a question. Before leaving, Elmer offered some advice, "Jimbo, I'd report it to someone who was closer to your house or ask them if they saw it also. On second thought, I'd call the state police or the sheriff." They both knew Elton and wondered whether Jim was getting a little nervous as he left the store and remained uncertain as to the next step. He considered chucking the entire chain of events, thankfully he remained steadfast.

With the gasoline secured in the bed of his pick-up, he didn't pay much attention to the farms he was passing, he kept mulling over what he saw earlier. He deduced what it wasn't. About 2 miles north of his home, as he drove up a crest in the road he spotted some strange marks. At 40 miles an hour he couldn't distinguish what they were or what caused them. He knew they weren't skid marks. He quickly turned the volume down lowering the country and western music so he could concentrate better. Slowing down and leaning forward, grasping the steering wheel for a better look, they didn't become any more familiar. They made a U turn and went off the east side of the road, onto a shoulder and then returned in the direction he was headed.

Weaver picked up the trail like a Walker Hound chasing a snowshoe rabbit. Lurching forward, they didn't become any more visible. He was careful not to crush, whatever it was, with his wheels. He was sure he was on to something. The state police would soon tell him what he saw, but only after he became a person of interest. They would aim at the messenger but wouldn't shoot him.

James returned the tractor without the wildest notion what was in store for the next three days, filled with questions, accusations and having his home converted into a temporary precinct.

Chapter 2

The Others

It was 10:a.m., April 26, 1973. Dorothy Stanco was on her way to Griffiss Air Force Base in Rome, N.Y.to shop at the Commissary and Base Exchange. As the wife of a retired Navy man, it was a well deserved benefit after having been alone for birthdays, holidays and anniversaries for many years. She was a clever shopper and enjoyed the prices compared with other stores. She'd grocery shop at the Commissary and then go to the Exchange to return a pair of trousers she had bought for her fast growing son. She was alone as she headed down Gorge Road, not far from Steuben.

The roads were dry, clouds blocking the sun and high 40's. She called her route "The back way" and wouldn't chance it in the winter. The forecast was clear and dry. She had plenty of time and was reveling in the expectation of an early spring and the thoughts of restocking her pantry and refrigerator. She knew the right size pants would make her son happy.

Leaving her home in White Lake a half hour earlier in order to get to the Base at the time the stores open, she had nothing to distract her. She had a full breakfast and remembered the adage, never shop on an empty stomach.

As she headed west she saw a green car, later described as greenish-blue. Having a penchant for colors she knew her vision was accurate. Her uncertainty of the make wasn't as accurate, saying it was either a Chevrolet or Plymouth. She did know that there was a hub cap missing on the right rear wheel. Her labeling was to be crucial. The car was parked on the south side of the road, "Kinda' facing towards me, backed into a parking area." The car was empty.

She was six or seven minutes from Potato Hill Road when she spotted the car. Her suspicion wasn't jarred as this was a favorite spot for fishermen to leave their car and trout season had just opened. The area was tagged as, Old Black River.

Finishing her errands and after returning home, she dismissed her picture of the parked car. A few days later, a newspaper article piqued her memory as she read about the homicide in Steuben, close to where she saw the green-bluish car parked with the missing hub cap. She called the Remsen Station of the state police and reported her observation. They carefully included her call in the blotter.

Mrs. Stanco wasn't the only car in the vicinity that morning, Joyce Broadbent was nearby also, at about the same time frame. Joyce was cautious, bordering on being slightly compulsive. She washed her car often, even in the cold weather, to prevent the salt on the roads from pitting the finish. She also had a familiarity with the narrow roads in the area of Steuben. The shoulders weren't uniform and the frost had heaved the macadam in certain spots. She liked to maintain her speed at around 35. She was adamant about the time, it was 10 to 10:30, Thursday, April 26, 1973. She came forward with the unnerving incident details, as did Mrs. Stanco, when the story broke about the body being found near Potato Hill.

The coincidence of the time and description supported Dorothy's testimony and the conclusion of their stories would mesh- they saw the same car. Mrs. Broadbent was on Route 274 that runs east and west, Remsen to the east and Frenchville to the west. She was headed in the same direction as Dorothy, west. She said she was about a half mile from Frenchville and was negotiating a curve in the road and slowing down. She steered as close to the right edge of the road as she dared, to allow any unseen, oncoming cars, enough room to pass safely. She was close to where Dorothy saw the parked car. An oncoming car caused her to swerve to the right and gauged the encroaching vehicle to be going "Twice my speed." Passing safely but perilously, she shouted "You idiot!" Shaken but poised enough to recall the speeders car, she knew it was greenish-blue, matching Dorothy's account.

Looking in the rear view mirror, she followed the path of the driver that enraged her, to get a second look. She described the driver as "White male, medium length hair, bearded, in his 30's, sat high in the seat and alone." Her description included, "Never looked at me, damn fool!" Her eye for detail helped her refine her recounting of the close

7

call. She said, "The rear tail lights were oblong, not square, not round, oblong. I'm not sure about the make but I know what it wasn't, a Ford or Chevy. He had a trailer hitch and I'm sure I saw a piece of rope dangling from the ball on the hitch." Following the passing car in the mirror would be critical.

She'd become a prosecutors ideal witness, positive, unflappable and disinterested. The type that a defense attorney wouldn't dare to cross examine and he didn't. Ted Wolff couldn't wait to make her one of his lead testifiers.

Chapter 3

SIGHTINGS

Steve Earl had mixed emotions about spring arriving. Sure he'd be outside more, closer to vacation time but he faced cleaning up the residue of the winter. He worked for ENCON, New York State Department of Environmental Conservation, a member of the Green Team. He'd never admit to liking his job, but with five kids and turning forty in June, he enjoyed the security. The huge plus was that he liked the guys in his crew, Earl Winters and Joe Kozick.

Winters was the boss, but only on paper. They all worked equally so the hierarchy was only obvious in the paychecks. The weather controlled their schedule and on Thursday, April 26, 1973, it rained until an hour before noontime. The crew puttered around in the storehouse in Hawkinsville and when it cleared they decided to set out for Steuben, to clean up the state land along Latteiman Road. Steve and Earl were in the four wheel drive Ford pick-up, Kozick drove the Travelall. They traversed the Hogback Road to State Route 12, then to Potato Hill Road and took a right onto Latteiman, arriving. as they recall, at 11:45 a.m. It was approaching, what they called dinner time, but Steve was less than anxious about another baloney sandwich on white.

On their way they waved to a pair of state workers pruning sagging maple tree limbs on Potato Hill Road. Latteiman would fit the description of a lane rather than a road. They scanned the sides of the road as they decided to go to the cul-de-sac and work their way back to Potato Hill.

The open meadow on the left ran for about a half mile before it joined the wooded section. As they approached the tree area, Winters saw a car approaching. He slowed down cautiously and hoped there'd be enough clearance. They were close to a section called the Hardwood Plantation. The narrow gravel road could be treacherous, open ditches

9

and four feet deep, with no guide rails. Winters described the oncoming car as, "Shiny, dark-green, Chrysler product, maybe a Plymouth, fairly new with wide front tires. The driver was alone, late 20's-early 30's, long hair, dark complexion and a mustache." As the state trucks passed the car, no one waved.

They stopped at noon, carefully stowing their sandwich wraps and napkins in their lunch pails. The passing car wasn't discussed during their break. At 12:30, Kozick announced, "Saddle-up," and they started to walk to the Plantation.

While posting, "No trespassing" signs, Winters yelled, "There's drag marks on the road!" They were in the cul-de-sac, about 2/3 around the loop and in the middle of the road and there were remnants of a fire. The ashes were cold and scattered as if it was intentional.

Steve bent over and started to pick through the soot. He lifted, what appeared to be a woman's shoe. A heel was missing with protruding nails where it was attached. Raking with their gloved hands, they uncovered a handbag, lined with red nylon. A sheet from what they surmised was from a woman's magazine as the page had a recipe, was also in the ashes. They placed the remains of a shoe, the handbag and the scraps from the magazine into a plastic bag and tossed it in the bed of the pick-up to be dumped later.

Working their way back to Potato Hill, they picked up beer and soda cans, bottles and fast food wrappers. The dry weather remained, but overcast. Other than the passing car they didn't encounter another soul except a fisherman parked along the road. They didn't ask whether he saw the drag marks.

About two o'clock, Weaver drove past his home, took a right on Latteiman and spotted the ENCON crew close to the Plantation. He knew them as they often parked their trucks on his land when they worked close by. They knew James also. Parking his truck near them, Weaver opened the conversation with, "Saw somethin' dragged on the Hill this mornin'. You guys see anythin'? " It was an impolite greeting, but then, they thought, that's Weaver. The three strolled over to his truck, silently, waiting for more details. Weaver leaned his capped head half way out of the window, rested his elbow on the door and declared, "Shiny car with somethin' draggin' from a rope behind it." The crew looked at each other waiting for someone to answer. Winters finally said, "Nope, nothing like that. We did find a lady's shoe and a handbag." One of the crew said, "Maybe somebody got rid of their old lady." The other two giggled but Weaver didn't join in their humor. Winter added, "Saw a guy fishing, came up empty, streams too high, waters still cold." Weaver didn't fish and wouldn't tolerate being called a sportsman. His farm and cattle occupied his life.

Weaver asked, "What did you do with that shit you found?" Someone said, "Bagged it," pointing to the back of one of the trucks. James dismounted from his truck, pointing to the meadow and directed their attention to the matted weeds in the overgrown area behind where they were standing. The crew wondered if they missed some trash. "See that area? Looks funny doesn't it? All tramped down, looks to me like a person got dragged. See the tire marks and they ain't been there a helluva long time." They did appear different and didn't blend.

The conversation was anything but fluid, marked with-Uh-Hu- and –I see. Nothing current, global or mind taxing, but hinged on what was seen, found, and what could it be or mean. Winters said to James, "We saw a car, come to think of it, going toward the Plantation. Almost forced me off the road, thought I was going in the ditch. This road isn't safe for two vehicles to pass safely. I inched over so he could get by. Didn't get a good look at him except I know he was alone."

James started toward his truck thinking that the crew wasn't much help. Standing next to his truck, he put both hands to the peak of his cap and shouted back, "Hey-the drag marks are going back, like it looped!" They were headed in the direction of Potato Hill Road, took a left and in the direction of his house.

Kozick walked to the T intersection of Potato Hill and Latteiman with Weaver two steps behind. Staring at the macadam, they agreed the marks were left by an object and pulled along the pavement. Weaver exclaimed, "By the Jesus, they look like testines." Kozick assented to Weavers conclusion but left some doubt when he answered, "If you say so, Jim." The brownish-yellow matter resembled intestines, whether animal or human would be the call of/for the experts. Trooper R. Gallo would later frame them as "Chicken fat." Kozick waved to Winters for a second opinion. Bending over, Winters, with one knee on the pavement, placed his index finger on the glob and as if he was lifting frosting from an iced cake and brought it to his nose. He rose, extended his finger towards Kozick and said, "Here, you sniff it. Smells like beef."

An opinion wasn't volunteered as they returned to their trucks and prepared to get back to Hawkinsville and punch out. They did take one more glance at the pasture where the weeds were flattened. There was no correlation between the marks on the road and the grassy area. They had some doubts about Mr. Weaver's lesson in anatomy and didn't know him well enough to make a judgment as to his sobriety. They didn't know Elton either.

For the state workers, the remainder of the day was routine, deposit the trash in a dumpster to include the shoe, handbag and ripped magazine page. They didn't share the statement about the "Old Lady" with their wives nor did they know how momentous their day would become.

Chapter 4

THE ODD COUPLE

Weaver decided to call the state police in Oneida, Troop D Headquarters. It was 2:30 in the afternoon, five hours after he saw something being dragged behind a car. Knowing full well that it was a long distance call he felt it was his duty to go public. Ten years later he would have the benefit of a cell phone.

He was bemused when he said, "Can't make a local call from my house. Can you believe that shit? If I had a phone in the cellar and I was in the parlor and someone called either way, It'd still be long distance." He thought about blaming the Arabs but couldn't make the connection.

The veteran civilian dispatcher at troop headquarters was Joseph Haug. Responding to the call, he answered, "Troop D Oneida, State Police, Mr. Hague." Weaver's response had the same directness as the dispatcher's, "Weaver, Steuben, give me someone to talk to." Mr. Haug thought he should have recognized the voice by Weaver's tone, but he didn't. Asking for details, Weaver filled in the blanks, "Saw somethin' bein' dragged behind a car right on the road in front of me." The report was nebulous and Hague reacted by asking the standard questions, who, what, when and where so he could direct the call. Joe called it, "Separating the chaff from the grain." His response to the caller was, "Mr. Weaver, I'll have someone get right back to you if you'll leave a number where we can contact you."

James recited his schedule when he'd be available and reminded the dispatcher that it's a long distance call and hoped he wouldn't have to call Oneida again. He said he'd need an hour to care for his cows and said he didn't have a phone in the barn. James wasn't happy about the response from headquarters. His patience ran out when he didn't get a call and reluctantly called back at about 5:00 p.m..

Not recognizing the evening dispatcher's voice he said, "Weaver again, Steuben!" He felt he was being patronized when the dispatcher told him that a troop car was dispatched and should be there momentarily. Thanks and gratitude were expressed for being a concerned citizen but Weaver felt neglected and that he was being lied to. He was angry, grumbling to himself about how he adjusted his routine, hurrying through the milking and asking his wife to feed him supper earlier than usual. As his bedtime approached, about 8:30 in the evening, he decided to make his third call of the day. "Weaver, third call today, haven't seen a trooper with a big hat yet. It's 8:30 and nobody's showed." His reaction was met with the promise, "Mr. Weaver, I'm in radio contact with the trooper in your zone and by the time you hang up the phone he'll be rapping on your door." Weaver lost his politeness and shouted "Bull Shit" and slammed the phone down.

Trooper Jon Chaffee preferred working C line, three to eleven p.m. He thought of it as the "Action Tour" and it was. He was able to see his kids during the day, before and after school. After a short stint with the B.C.I. he returned to road patrol and felt that was more to his liking. He was nearing retirement and anxious to start a new career. He not only knew the rural map, he knew the territory. He knew the predisposition of the "Bad Guys" and their habits and patterns. The call to Weaver's house was the most unusual night of his career.

Proceeding to Steuben, he was directed by the garbled message to interview a witness who said he saw something being dragged behind a car earlier that day. He knew the Potato Hill area but the houses weren't numbered, only the mail boxes at the edge of the driveways. Weaver gave the dispatcher a benchmark when he said, "I'll have my new truck at the end of the driveway." The truck was three years old but new to Weaver.

In a few minutes but too long for James, Chaffee found the house and spotted the white pick-up parked in the driveway. If there weren't lights on in the house, he would have imagined it was vacant. Responding to the rap on the door, Weaver's indelicate greeting was, "Where have you been? Forget my age and all that other shit, it's dusk and I want you to see my find." Chaffee understated his feeling when he called Weaver "Rude."

After a quick summary of what he saw, Weaver was invited to take a ride with the trooper and eased himself into the front seat of the grey and white troop car, a Crown Victoria. He felt in control and directed Chaffee to turn and go south on Potato Hill Road. After a few hundred feet, Weaver commanded, "Stop right here, hold it." Pulling the cruiser to the right shoulder and putting the flashing lights on for safety, Chaffee wondered what was next. Weaver said, "Want to show you the marks left by the draggin.'"

They walked the few feet to where the conversation took place with the ENCON crew earlier that day. There were no street lights to illuminate the desolate road. Looking at the smudge Chaffee's reaction was that it was road kill. Weaver began the conversation with the trooper aiming the flashlight to the unidentified matter and said, "What do you think? You're the law, you should know what it is!" Chaffee's response was open and added, "Can't tell Mr. Weaver," as he thought of the courtesy code of the state police.

James chimed in with a supposition, "Looks like inwards to me, sure as hell. Learned that in the U.S. Army." The trooper was within a heartbeat of saying to his partner, "Shut the f--- up Mr. Weaver, let me make up my own mind." Chaffee had the reputation of possessing a disarming tone in his voice and the more crass a person became the more pleasant and polite he was. The trooper responded to Weaver's determination and said, "We'll dispatch this to our tissue analyst in Albany and an opinion will be rendered after microscopically determining whether it is human or animal. A professional opinion will be rendered and the results forwarded, that will be sustained through the most rigid cross examination." Weaver thought that was a long answer for such a short and simple question.

James suggested they follow the markings on the road. Chaffee said that the lack of street lights would make it difficult. Weaver convinced his new found buddy to drive down Latteiman Road where Weaver had huddled with the ENCON group earlier. Chaffee was concerned that he might lose a muffler because of the elevated crown in the dirt road and steered to the opposite lane with the right wheels on the crown. They stopped where the marks left the road and entered the meadow. Walking to the weeded area with the flashlight as the beacon, Chaffee felt unnerved as he wondered whether James was unpredictable and could become unglued. The shrill sound of a bird provoked another disagreement, Waver saying it was an owl, Jon stating it was a mourning dove. Weaver ended the dispute when he said, "No struggle here, leaves ain't taken up, still down and tight."

Chaffee adjusted his grey jacket and followed the beaten path and James followed mumbling to himself. Tugging at the troopers belt to get his attention, he said, "Got it figured. That shiny green car that I saw draggin' something' made two loops out there in the meadow. Whoever it was that was drivin' stripped the clothes off of the body, turned around at that there elm and came back around again."

The messenger had ruled out the prospect of the "Thing" being a dog, cat or raccoon. His reasoning was that if it was an animal they would have sent a Humane Officer, not a trooper to investigate. Chaffee remained ambivalent about what he saw. If it was a false report, why three insistent phone calls? His thought of arresting Weaver for a false report was dispelled when he stumbled on what appeared to be part of a rope, maybe a clothes line. It appeared to have blood and hair on it. He cautiously bagged it and returned to the car.

Accepting Weaver's suggestion to visit the cul-de-sac, they found nothing significant there and returned to Potato Hill Road. His low beams picked up something on the pavement and he aimed his side beam light and then pulled over to the shoulder. They walked to the specimen and it was a sizeable chunk of innards. Recovering a knife from the trunk Chaffee knelt next to the hunk of matter and scraped carefully the find, scooping it into the sweat band of his Stetson.

Weaver asked, "What's the story on the rope you picked up in the meadow? Looks like it's long enough to make a noose around someone's neck. It's busted off, you know, probably longer earlier." Chaffee's patience was depleted as he pointed his index finger at the witness, raised his voice and said, "You read too many God-dam detective books Mr. Weaver." His reply was, "Shit. I don't read no kinda' books."

The pro-tem relationship was soon to wind down with the initial stages of investigation completed. They returned to Weaver's cluttered kitchen and sat at a table as the trooper began his report. James described the questioning when he said, "He took everythin' 'cept my temperature." He had no appreciation of the administrative requirements of police agencies.

It was a wearying day for James, but satisfied in the notion that he did the right thing by calling the state police. He couldn't forecast what tomorrow held in store for him.

Chaffee called Sergeant Roman, said he was back in service and grateful he got rid of the pesky messenger and reported what he thought was nebulous findings, stowed in his head gear. He was told to return to the New Hartford office with the evidence and the report of his interview and Roman would make the decision as to pursue or drop it.

Roman elected to take the next step, send it to the Lab in Albany immediately. At 5:30 the next morning, Trooper Art Broccoli was dispatched to hand carry the evidence to Albany, wait for the results and relay the conclusion to Roman. The ninety mile one way drive was frightening but redeeming for James Weaver, the positive identification was that it was human tissue. The investigation took a giant step.

Chapter 5

The Victim

Mary Rose (nee Byrnes) Turner was a modest soul, required very little attention and unpretentious. She had her family, a few favored friends and many acquaintances. She was a secretary at the Oneida County Civil Services Office and was described as responsible. Her year old Chevrolet Nova had logged 6,000 miles, suggesting a degree of mobility. She rented a comfortable four room flat from her two elderly landlords, Louise 81 and her brother Frank Jenny. Frank was a year younger than his sister. The Jenny's characterized her as the ideal tenant, paid her rent promptly for five years, but eccentric at times

She was a faithful member of the Rosary Society at St. Joseph's-St. Patrick's Catholic Church. Although divorced, she always wore her wedding band and her family said she carried a set of rosary beads with her. The conventional appearance shielded her disturbed inner self. She had the classic symptoms of an anxious person: insomnia attacks, occasional disorientation, depression, absenteeism and at times, irrationality. In the fall of 1970, she went swimming alone, in the darkness, at Hinckley Reservoir, 19 miles from her home. After the swim she walked aimlessly through the woods. Such episodes caused her to become institutionalized at the Utica Psychiatric Center. She failed at suicide attempts, causing worry for her children, brothers and sisters.

After a routine week at work and the weekend with nothing scheduled, she decided to embark on an adventure to Albany, 90 miles East of Utica. It was April 21, 1973.

With enough cash and her rosary beads in her purse, she set out on a jaunt. In a clear but chilly morning she left her driveway at 4:15, hoping not to disturb the Jenny's.

Interstate 90, the Thomas E. Dewey Thruway, wasn't busy that morning. Tractor trailers and a few vacationers were the only people on the road. As she drove within the 50 mile per hour limit she fantasized about the possibility of visiting a widower named Percy. She had difficulty bringing up his last name. Percy lived in the Capital City and she hadn't seen him in many years. She even thought of the possibility of a relationship of sorts, being in the cards. Exiting 24, the first of two Albany ramps, she decided to look for a motel. She ended up on Central Avenue and looked for refuge in a fairly decent, inexpensive lodging. She caught sight of a neon sign with the vacancy sign lit. She was comforted as the sign said, phone/TV. She thought that she may end up calling Percy.

She booked a room, signed the register, make and plate number of her Nova and the night auditor, as the want ads call them, directed her to room 3. Her license tag was UZ3197. Raymond Kelly was the night clerk and gave her change for the twenty dollar bill, handing her a five and 2 pennies.

Kelly gave her the room closest to the office as he instinctively thought she might need something. He never realized the importance of giving her the key to room 3, nor the value of her not returning the key to the desk as she left. Before she left for her room, Kelly offered her a cup of coffee that had been brewing since he arrived at work, midnight. She graciously declined saying she had stopped for a cup of tea on the Thruway. Kelly recalled her visit saying, "She walked from her car to room 3, no luggage, went in the room, came out and walked to her car, getting a small package."

The auditor had an unobstructed view of her room and he knew she didn't have any visitors while he was on duty. His relief was Mr. Waddell, arriving at 7:a.m. He supported Kelly's statement that she didn't have visitors. Waddell saw Mrs. Turner, at about 8:00 a.m., backing out of the parking space. He matched the car with the register and thought she may be going to the nearby mall or visit someone. His curiosity wasn't aroused, lots of clients just stop and spruce up and then leave. Her room was paid for until 11:00 a.m. the next day. When Waddell returned the following day, he didn't realize she had left without leaving her key either at the desk or in the door. Kelly picked it up on the night shift. room 3 was cleaned on early afternoon, Sunday,

April 22. A tooth brush and a pair of panties were placed in lost and found by the maid.

Kelly noted that the bed was slept in, no calls were made, local or long distance, no incoming or outgoing. The records showed card number 18470, only the second occupancy since January 1, 1973. No one was to know what occurred during the hour she spent in the room, she may have said the rosary.

Mary Rose returned to Utica and called her son Clyde who lived in Syracuse. She told him she was going to Buffalo and he said it was 10 in the morning when she phoned, seemingly shortly after arriving if she had left Albany at 8. Clyde didn't ask his mother, she didn't volunteer the reason. She never mentioned her trip to Albany.

Mary Rose took a slight detour on her trip west and stopped at her daughter's home in East Syracuse, but not finding her there, she left a note. Continuing to Buffalo, she spent the night with friends, saying she's going to Syracuse and couldn't stand the traffic in a large city.

Her priest didn't see her at mass Sunday and she called in sick on Monday. For some unknown reason, she was westbound on the Thruway at 6:30 p.m., Monday. She had stopped at the service area near milepost 210, called Indian Castle. She had stopped for gas and the attendant, Elmer Pflanz, was working the pumps. Elmer was to the rear of Mary Rose's car and in front of the car behind her. Mary Rose couldn't explain why she did it, but suddenly she put her Nova in reverse and sandwiched Mr. Pflanz's legs between the two bumpers. She was apologetic and started to cry. The Troop T Station was next door to the accident and an ambulance hurried Elmer to the nearest hospital, Little Falls, with back and leg injuries. Trooper Dodge tried to console Mrs. Turner and was gracious enough not to ticket her, using his discretion.

Clyde's concern for his mother's mental health was elevated on Tuesday the 24th when he received a distress call about 8 in the evening. His mother was calling from the Northway Inn outside of Syracuse and asked for intercession, as she said she couldn't find her glasses and could he come and help her find them. Arriving in the parking lot, Clyde found her distraught, gripping the steering wheel and eyes blazing. Clyde figured his mom has lost it, after he found the glasses on the front seat. He masked his impatience, feeling more sympathy than ire. He didn't have an inkling as to where she had been between early Saturday morning until Tuesday night. He loved his mother deeply but he was approaching being exasperated.

Mary Ann, her daughter, also lived nearby, in East Syracuse. Clyde asked his mother to follow him to Mary Ann's house, where she would convince her to stay overnight. The loving daughter and son, Mary Ann and Clyde, shared an enmity for their father, but considered their mother to being close to a saint, although an erratic one. They concurred that she wasn't in any condition to drive back to Utica.

Mary Rose suffered through a restless night, feeling guilty for displacing her grandchildren from their bedroom She felt she was getting more caring attention than she deserved. She fell asleep reciting the Glorious Mysteries of the Rosary. She had said earlier that they were much happier than the Sorrowful decade.

The next day she ruminated, somewhat incoherent at times, but agreeable and glad she had the security of her children tending to her. Mary Ann, with difficulty, grounded her mother. It was painful as she thought of the adage, "One mother can take care of five children-five children can't take care of one mother." She was doing what she felt was best for all concerned. Mary Ann recommended that her mother restrict her driving, just for a while.. Agreeing to drive her mother's car to Utica and have Clyde follow her, Mary Rose appeared relieved. They both knew their mother had an appointment with a psychiatrist the next Saturday but didn't know of the mishap at the gas pump. Mary Ann parked the Nova in the Jenny's driveway and took the only set of keys with her. It was the last time she would see her mother alive. She kissed her as she left, and said, "I love you Mom."

Clyde called his mother on Wednesday night and reminded her that he'd be in Utica Saturday to take her to the doctor's.. He found her glib, upbeat and optimistic. "See you Saturday Mom, have a good night's sleep.' Those were his last words to his mother.

Mrs. Turner had many acquaintances, but one close friend, a co-worker, Viola Dwyer. She was her confidant. They developed a close relationship, riding the bus together to work. Mary Rose seldom drove to work, a mile from her house in the County Office Building since parking could be a problem. She also looked forward to visiting with Viola. On rare occasions when she drove she'd pick up Viola two blocks away. Mary Rose trusted her enough to share intimacies that included stories about her divorced husband's abuse. Viola was the only person who knew that, outside of her family.

Whether it was a ruse resulting from fear and loneliness, Mary Rose would sometimes seek refuge for the night at Viola's home, saying, she misplaced her keys. Viola was also privy to her fascination with Percy. Viola said she thought his last name was Kennedy and that he was an uncle of Mary Rose's daughter-in-law, but wasn't quite sure.

Shortly before Viola left for the bus on Wednesday morning, about 7:45, Mary Rose called and said that she wasn't coming to work that day and to tell her supervisor she was ill. Viola got a call on Wednesday night and knew it was Mary Rose as she greeted her friend with, "Hi dear. I'm having gall bladder surgery and I'm tired of driving so I gave Mary Ann my car." Viola told her how everyone misses her at work and want her to get better. She didn't have any gossip to pass on. Mary Rose told her how appreciative she is of Clyde and Mary Ann and how fortunate she is and didn't deserve their concern. Mary Rose said she'd be to work Thursday and she thought she'd go to bed early as she had a slight headache. Viola wasn't surprised when her friend wasn't on the bus Thursday.

The Jenny's were like family to Mrs. Turner, sharing the same distress as her children over her stability. Mary Ann had rapped on their door when she took her home and removed her keys and told them her mother wouldn't be driving for awhile. She told the landlords how much she appreciated their care. As Mary Ann left, she said , "Keep an eye on Mom for us."

Three hours before their ritual of watching the 11 o'clock news and then retiring, they asked Mary Rose to have a couple of hands of cards. Mary Rose declined, said she was tired and went upstairs.

Satisfied that the garbage had been placed neatly next to the curb for an early pick up, Frank Jenny had dozed off when their door bell rang. He was the designated gatekeeper after dark. Muttering to himself as he tried to find the sleeve in his bathrobe, he shuffled to the front door. Louise was awakened and eavesdropped, more curious than frightened. Frank pulled the door curtain to one side, peeking out before opening it. Mary Rose was recognized , standing in the 40 degree weather without a coat, sweater or shawl. He opened the door.

She said she was sorry to bother him and said she forgot her key and needed to get a coat. Being grounded, he wondered where she was going, particularly after saying she was too tired to play cards.

Louise got up and stood behind her brother, thinking she'd be a little more diplomatic if there was a spat. She didn't hear her come down the stairs before the bell rang and wondered if she was outside without a coat. Frank, with a modest gesture, closed his bathrobe and cinched the cloth belt tightly, covering his flannel pajamas. Not questioning his tenant, he retrieved her key from the buffet. Walking outside to the upstairs door, the street light allowed him to find the key hole without his glasses. He turned to Mary Rose and asked, "Where are you going this time of night?" Her answer was out of character, as she reacted, "I don't have to tell you where I'm going or who I'm going with." Frank walked back inside and mumbled "Why do I put up with her crap."

Listening for the next move, the Jenny's heard Mrs. Turner stomp down the stairs, slam the door and walk off the front porch in a strident manner. Louise stayed up for a short time, Frank returned to his bed, sulking.

Directly across the street on the southeast corner of Noyes Street, was Friedel's Funeral Home, neatly manicured and the finest house in the neighborhood. It was completely dark. Mary Rose stood in front of it, conspicuously for this time of night, especially with her red coat. Louise returned to the front window looking at the Funeral Home, in darkness, in order to avoid being seen. Mrs. Turner was silhouetted against the street light. Her surveillance lasted about twenty minutes and wondered what was in the plastic purse she was grasping. She began walking east toward the bus stop on Court Street. Louise returned to her bed, ruffled by her friend, tenant and sometimes card player.

The landlords slept soundly and didn't hear Mary Rose return. The only odd occurrence the next morning was the garbage cans and their placement. They were emptied and placed in the rear of their house. Frank had left the cans on the curb and never remembers the trash collectors leaving them anywhere except the curb and he concluded that Mary Rose had returned them on her way to work. They would never see their neighbor again to get an answer.

Two doors east of Friedel's lived Richard and Clarice Fox and they were also having a restless night. They had taken a trip to Albany, leaving at 6:a.m.and returning home 12 hours later. They retired earlier than normal, nine o'clock. Clarice woke up at 3:15 a.m. and out of habit, walked to the front window facing Court Street. She had a clear view of the area and recognized Mary Rose standing alone on the front porch of the Jenny's house. She was pawing in her purse, acting as if she was trying to find something. Clarice thought she was looking for her keys, either for the car or the door. She called her husband to the window and they agreed it was unusual, but living a block from the Utica Psychiatric Center, they had seen stranger behavior. A later interview recited that the only glaring observation they had was the red coat, nothing else. They returned to bed thinking that she's an adult and they shouldn't spy any longer.

A mile east and downhill from Mary Rose's flat was a Shell Gas Station , owned and operated by Harold Bohling. It was on the southwest corner of State and Court Streets, full service and one of the few all night stations in downtown Utica. Mary Rose wasn't a regular customer and the only dealing she had with Bohling's was in August, 1972, that could be documented. She said she had charged $5.00 worth of gas, let it slide without paying, but had some guilt feelings when she was a patient in St. Elizabeth's Hospital on the third floor, the psychiatric section. When an acquaintance, Julia Swider, visited her in the hospital she asked Julia to pay the outstanding bill and gave her five dollars and directions to the station. Julia agreed and delivered the money. Julia said Mrs. Turner's delinquency was the result of a check that bounced, not charged.

There's an offbeat mix of people on the streets in Utica after midnight. In late April, pedestrians are uncommon. Some motorists, bar employees, customers, insomniacs, police patrol cars and taxis are around, but few walkers, especially lone females. It's not Times Square at 3:00 a.m. Mary Rose was remembered by the nocturnal group that saw her, as being abnormal.

Mary Rose walked down the hill towards the station, tipping over garbage cans and shouting at the passing cars in a frenzied way.

Anthony Corelli and two of his pals, Ray Secor and Bob Cable, were part of her audience. They had been "On the town" and Corelli needed gas before going home to Hinckley, sixteen miles north. They said it was about two thirty and that a young man tended them at the pumps. Corelli and Secor went inside, to the bay or pit area, to put air in a bicycle tire as Cable stayed in the car. They noticed a car on the hoist and an employee was working on a gas tank. A man, whom they thought was the customer, described as "Big," was watching the procedure. A female, "Sloppy looking, wearing white shorts," was walking around the car as it was being worked on..

As Corelli left the station, after the tank was filled and air put in the bicycle tire, he stopped at the sidewalk to allow a pedestrian to pass. She was going toward the pumps and the driver rolled his window down as he tried an unveiled attempt at suggestion and said," Hey sweetheart, kinda' late for you to be out, isn't it?" His passengers chuckled and slapped their knees, but the female didn't respond and kept walking. She was depicted as, "Medium height and weight, late 30's-early 40's, wore a trench coat to her knees , glasses, medium length dark hair, alone and kept her hands in her pockets."

A restaurant owner in Clinton was returning to his home in West Utica and had some letters to mail. It was, as Ed Frey related, about 3:30 a.m., Thursday April 26, 1973. Stopping at a mail box near the station, as he left the curb, he saw a meandering woman who seemed to recognize him and thought, if he stopped she would have gotten in his car. He didn't stop and didn't know her name or face. He said she had a reddish trench coat, unbuttoned or unzipped, slacks, light colored, short hair, 5'-6", average build, 50 to 60, thought she was carrying an umbrella. Within four days, Mary Rose Turner, DOB 9/18/16, would be delicately unearthed and carefully removed from a superficial grave twenty miles northeast of where she was last seen and impossible to quickly identify with the exception of her hair strand and the lobe of one ear. Her body was massacred.

Weaver's home

CHARLES F. AIKEN
1920 – FATHER – 1951
DOROTHEA E. AIKEN
1924 – MOTHER – 1980
LINDA S. CADY
1947 – DAUGHTER – 1973
LISA ANN CADY
1966 – GRANDAUGHTER – 1973

Grave marker

Victim's grave

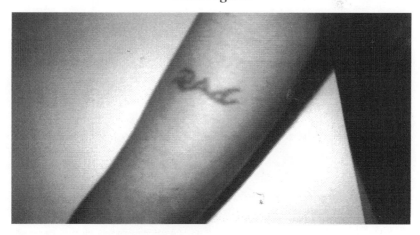

Cassandra Hatch left arm

OPAL RING OWNED BY M.R. TURNER
EXHIBIT 14 AT GRAVE SITE

CHARRED REMAINS AT CUL-DE-SAC
EXHIBIT 46

PROSECUTOR, EDWARD J (Ted) WOLFF Jr.

*CRIMINAL JUSTICE STUDENTS S.P. DOG & TROOPERS
SEARCHING WITH "PEARL", THE
N.Y.S.P. EVIDENCE DOG*

GRAVE SITE OFF LATTEIMAN ROAD
EXHIBIT 59

UNEARTHED GRAVE
EXHIBIT 54

CUL-DE-SAC BURNED MATERIAL ON LEFT
EXIBIT 44

"T" INTERSECTION LATTEIMAN & POTATO HILL RDS
EXHIBIT 30

LOOKING NORTH ON POTATO HILL RD
DRAG-MARKS IN BOTH LANES
EXHIBIT 35

LATTEIMAN RD. NEAR GRAVE SITE

AERIAL VIEWS OF SEARCHED REGION PHOTO
TAKEN BY U-2
EXHIBIT 109

LOOKING NORTH ON POTATO HILL RD
DRAG MARKS
EXHIBIT 37

THE COMMAND POST

MARY ROSE TURNER'S STEUBEN GRAVE

OPENING TO GRAVE SITE

GLOB ANALYZED AS HUMAN MATTER

BODY DRAG MARKS AND DIRECTION REVERSED

Chapter 6

THE WITNESS

After Thursday's bizarre occurrences, James had a fitful night, tossing and turning from midnight to 5 a.m. when he tended to his herd. Mrs. Weaver left for work at the psych center and gave little credence to her husband's report and conclusion as to what was being dragged. Weaver groused to her about what he felt was shabby treatment by Trooper Chaffee. The feeling was mutual. She had heard the long distance complaint often. She wasn't consoling, and as Weaver said, "She was half listenin'" She'd escape the commotion of Friday.

With the early morning chores over, he returned to the kitchen for his second cup of coffee when the phone rang. "Mr. Weaver, State Police, New Hartford." His response was a pithy, "Yep. Go on." The caller continued, "Mr. Weaver, would you be willing to go out to the road and the meadow with us again and explain and show us what you saw yesterday?" Evidence and observation require continuity, repetition, perception and they usually determine whether the witness is unswerving and constant. His testimony would be unvarying and rote. He agreed, but with provisions, "Got to get my chores done first, I'll go after, at my convenience. Sure you don't mind."

Sergeant Roman, the caller, shared his notes that recited his reaction. "Trooper Chaffee, Thursday at 10 p.m., called me at the Remsen Station and wanted to meet me there. He discussed Weaver's observations earlier that day and thought that the intestines, rope and hair were human. I contacted Captain George Chromey at the Oneida Barracks and he directed that arrangements be made to have the evidence sent to the S.P. Lab in Albany, in order to arrive at 7 a.m. on the 27th. Trooper Broccoli left for the Lab at 5:30 the following morning. At 7 a.m. on the 27th, Chaffee ,along with Sgt. Romaine Gallo, went to the scene to photograph the drag marks on Potato Hill

Road, as we were sure it was gong to rain that morning and feared that the marks would disappear. It was a dreary, overcast day and quite cold. We found the scene as Chaffee had described the night before. We found more pieces of rope with what appeared to have blood and hair attached. We also found traces of the intestines along Latteiman Road, to the turn around. Someone had overturned several shovel sized lumps of soil with nothing underneath them. At the logging road less than a quarter mile down the Latteiman Road, we also found a large piece of rope with blood and hair attached and a cameo ring that had been spread apart making it obvious that it was forcibly removed. A pair of woman's yellow panties were also found. The assumption was that the dragging began in that area. The marks indicated that the body was dragged east on Latteiman Road, through the open field and then on to Potato Hill Road to a point north of Weaver's house. The body appeared to have been tossed into a ditch on the east side of the road as the car turned around. The assumption was that the body was hitched back up, dragged south on Potato Hill Road, past Weaver's again and then west on Latteiman Road to the cul-de-sac where the burned clothing was found by ENCON. At 9 a.m. while at the cul-de-sac, Joe Haug, via radio, said that all of the evidence forwarded to the Lab were positively identified as human-not animal. I told Haug to inform the Troop Commander and then contacted N.H. asking for a detail of troopers to be dispatched from the entire zone. Eight troopers reported at 11 a.m. in addition to Sr. Inv.T. Gallagher and several B.C.I. The rain stopped after 2 hours and all the drag marks disappeared as the roads dried with sun appearing. At the cul-de-sac, a motel key was found and a pair of prescription glasses. The burned clothing recovered appeared to be a pinkish sport type jacket, consumed by fire except for the lapels. A phone call was made to the motel and the key was identified to be from the last occupant, Mary Rose Turner. The detail was secured at dusk, 5 p.m. after searching the area with negative results. A decision was made to continue the search the next day and that the Steuben Town Garage would be the Command Post. A chain was used to secure the entrance to Latteiman Road with the inscription,' Keep out-Crime Scene Search Area. N.Y. State Police.' Two troopers were assigned, one in each car, to remain in the area with one at the cul-de-sac throughout the night to protect the scene until daylight. M.T. Roman, Sgt."

After the phone call asking him to revisit the scene, Weaver carped to himself about his agreement. "There I go again, cuttin' corners to finish so those bastards can take down more stuff. Maybe they'll really take my temperature this time."

It was the second day of the bittersweet relationship between the messenger and the S.P. At 11:06 a.m. a trooper appeared with a plain clothed investigator. Weaver, concerned about dinner at the stroke of 12, said, "It's late in the day, lets get goin' and do what you have to do." He was up for 6 hours and late morning is late in the day for James. He was irked when the rain erased most of the marks and thought that if they had responded when he first called the day before they'd have more evidence. After a sermon on the demands of farming, cost of gasoline, long distance phone calls and the mid-east hoodlums who caused it, he said, "I'll go with you guys, but get me back for dinner." James plopped his powerful body in the front seat, slamming the door hard. The investigator sat in the left rear, the uniformed trooper backed the squad car out to the road.

Weaver asked, as they went right on Latteiman Road, "You guys feelin' the pinch, you know gas the way it is, probably cuts down on your overtime. Here's where me and my buddy Chaffee found the inwards last night." Weaver pointed to where he met with the ENCON crew, where the rope was found and the matted area in the field, volunteering the same thesis he told Chaffee. They drove to the turnaround where the burned, discarded items were found.

Weaver was dressed to grovel in the mud, his bib overalls were ideal for this venture. The neatly pressed gray uniform wasn't the appropriate dress for the task. As the rain pelted them, the two officers got on their hands and knees and peered into a sluice pipe that ran the width of the gravel road. James asked for permission to get out of the car and join them. Hearing the car radio crackle to life with the results from the lab, Weaver said, "Hot dog! I was right on the god-dam money." It was as if he was redeemed and that it wasn't an animal. The investigators didn't find anything in the pipe.

Inviting James to return to his own house, the trio, without conversing, pulled into his driveway. He was stunned when he saw a bunch of state cars, unmarked, black walled tires and a whip antenna invading his property. Entering the back door, he said, "There they were, a whole group of B.C.I.'s sittin' at my f------ table. The D.A.'s guy, Wolff, big as life, and they start givin' me that Mr. Weaver shit again." He was noticeably outraged but glad his wife wasn't home to see it. He thought that Elton would have gone over the edge if he was there. He continued barking his discontent, "I couldn't believe that shit, set up an office in my kitchen. Galliker (Thomas Gallagher, Senior Investigator, B.C.I.) sat there with a f------ cigar that long" stretching his arms two feet apart in an exaggerated gesture. He had second thoughts about accepting the Agway guys advice to call the troopers. Continuing his rant, he said, "He kept droppin' his ashes on the kitchen floor, like the Godfather and he was on the phone constantly. I got pissed and said, They're all long distance from here, even if you call next door. I gotta' pay the bills, you know." Gallagher tried to neutralize the witness and said, "Don't worry Mr. Weaver, we'll take care of the bills, every last one, trust me sir." When he got the bill the following month, he was amazed and possibly disappointed. The only long distance calls listed were the three he made on Thursday. He didn't know how they did it, he figured they must have had a secret code. He was impressed by the mystery.

If Mr. Weaver was to be categorized it would seem he was a person of interest, not a suspect, but a class above witness, subject or complainant. During the questioning, not interrogation, the bureau trains their investigators, through in-service, seminars and conferences, on the latest techniques- what works and what fails. They are an elite group, mostly with bachelors degrees, many with masters and some law students. The discovery of the matter being human became an incident, the body find will advance to a homicide, and it wouldn't take too long to raise the bar.

James was a bit edgy, standing as the questions were posed and not delighted when they asked him his name three times. He was stuck on the tactic of the ashes being flicked on his floor as he bemoaned, "Here they are, at my f------ house, my kitchen and that guy with the long stogie trying to confuse me, playin' switch, Weaver-James, they'd say, and I'd say, no, James Weaver. After a while I hardly knew my own name."

Not completely satisfied with his answers, much less his attitude, an investigator asked him if he'd go to the headquarters to take a polygraph. Jim asked what it was and the response was: a lie detector. Polygraphists often call it a truth exam as most people pass.

Satisfied with their circular, non-accusatory explanation and questions and the reassurance it would only take a few minutes, he agreed. Ignoring his chores and wanting it ended and not worried about being truthful and accurate, he left. He wasn't concerned about leaving the doors unlocked or his wife being shocked by the intrusion. Escorted to the unmarked car he quickly went to the front seat for the third time in 20 hours. He described the trip to Oneida as an adventure. "Sat in the front seat again, zipped right along, felt like a big shot. The radio was on but they were talkin' in code so I wouldn't hear no secret stuff."

It's the preliminary, the warm up, that makes the polygraph so effective. Although Weaver said it was "Kinda' fun" most people don't see the humor in disclosure, feeling their in the confessional box. Knowing there were troopers on the other side of the one way mirror, Weaver tried to display his flare for humor by going to the mirror, wagging his tongue, putting his thumbs in his ear and wiggling his fingers. He continued with his escapade, "They finally strapped somethin' on my arms and this guy picks up four or five playin' cards and says, don't show us. It was like bein' at the Boonville Fair. I was happy but they was dead serious. Shuffle 'em, he said, so I did. They say to me, is this an ace of spades? It was but they told me to say it wasn't. So, now I know what they're up to, they want me to lie, so I did. Next card I look at is a jack of hearts and they ask, is this a jack of hearts, and I say, no-no. Magine lyin' and they know it? I'm thinkin' to myself, what bull shit. They speed me down to Oneida to lie to them."

The technician gets a reading when the subject is lying and then goes for the jugular. "Mr. Weaver, are there, or where there, any incidents in your life that you are ashamed of?" His negative answer apparently fell within the limits of truthfulness as the probe continued. "Did you actually see a car drag something or someone?"

He answered affirmatively and a little boastful, "Bet your ass I did!"

He passed the 10 question exam and removed any allegations of being delusional. A limited education is not an equation to being truthful. Weaver seemed requited when he said, "First exam I never had to study for." He was a stand up guy.

The witness, messenger, and unflappable testifier, was delivered to his home as he sat upright in the front seat. When he got home, the guy with the big cigar had left and the entourage had relocated to the Highway Department Garage to set up the Command Post. His wife was not impressed with her husband's crucial role in the discovery and conviction of the predator. The State Police were.

James had two stressful and trying days and went to bed feeling he did the right thing and sure that justice would prevail. He returned to his repetitive chores on Saturday. The excitement during the next few months, helicopters, troop cars everywhere, a National Guard Battalion activated and a U-2 flying overhead, didn't distract him from his chores, but satisfied that he had performed his duty. He became a poised, self assured, direct and brilliant testifier nineteen months later when he took the oath and molded his powerful frame into the witness chair.

Chapter 7

The Search

Supported by the analysis of the Lab of Chaffee's discovery as being human matter, the state police had passed the phase of reasonable suspicion and were approaching probable cause-there was a homicide and there were parts of a victim. There wasn't a preponderance of evidence but enough to conclude that a reasonable man could draw a conclusion that a killing took place, not accidental, not a suicide.

The hunt for the body began using deductive and inductive reasoning. Weaver was eliminated as a suspect following the polygraph, which was deductive, inductive would embrace brainstorming by the police for an M.O. (Method of Operation, Modus Operandi) of a person or persons who would possibly commit such a heinous act of dragging a victim in daylight behind their car. The investigators had the nagging question as to who would perform this in daylight and did they have a, "Catch me if you can," frame of mind. It was to be a difficult challenge.

Weaver's house was a temporary gathering place and there had to be a larger and more appropriate building to house the maps, weapons, devices and cars. Major Charland had few choices in such a remote area, quickly eliminating the Grange Hall and the Methodist Church. He singled out the Town Highway Garage, ample space, telephones, secure and semi-public. Troop cars swarmed to Steuben and every available trooper was deployed, arriving from Watertown to State Route 20, Herkimer to Auburn.

There were thousands of acres to be searched and Charland knew he needed assistance, trained personnel and equipment. The September 9, 1971 Attica Riot was fresh in his mind when eleven correction officers and civilians were killed. The sole advantage the state police had in Attica was that it was a confined area, Potato Hill was immense.

Most of the responding and delegated troopers were veterans of Attica. The major was described by some as "grizzly" others thought him as empathetic, understanding and a gutsy leader who would support his troops.

In addition to national security, the National Guard had a secondary duty and mission called civic action and assistance. The governor of all 50 states has the authority to activate the Guard in a time of natural or unnatural disasters, floods, hurricanes, wild fires or riots. The Guard had been called to assist in quelling the Attica Riot and Charland respected their abilities. Zone Sergeant M.T. Roman had a professional and personal association with the commander of the 104th M.P.Battalion, Major Evans. Roman ran his suggestion of support for the monumental search by Major Charland who quickly agreed. Roman spoke to Evans, Evans called the Division Commander who received permission from the governor and the Military Police were mobilized in Steuben.

Senior A.D.A. Ted Wolff was right in the middle of the Command Post activity, helping to orchestrate the tactics and planning. He always wanted to be one of the first responders at a major crime scene and never wanted to be given a case to prosecute without knowing it from the 'Get-Go," as he called it. He was used to being called from his home, late at night, or from his camp, He was the quintessential trial attorney and was depended upon by the D.A. Richard Enders. Sitting in the garage, he never realized he'd be embroiled in the longest trial of Oneida County's history, nineteen months later.

The Friday rain washed most of the marks off the roads but not all. Riding on the roof of a troop car, Investigator Michael Jasek held a 16 mm camera and preserved, on film, the stream of matter on the roads, Latteiman and Potato Hill. The trail of evidence measured 9.6 miles and the route was: Latteiman Road west to Potato Hill, north and then south on Potato Hill, the pressed weeds to the meadow and ended at the cul-de-sac. A road block was established at the T intersection of Latteiman and Potato Hill. The greeting to the hailed motorist was: "Sir/Madam," as they tipped the brim of their hat, glancing at the front and rear seats for anything unusual and in plain view. The questions were standard: "Do you travel this road frequently? Did you happen to see a shiny green car in the vicinity Thursday morning or early afternoon? Did you see anything behind a car being dragged that caught your attention? Thank you, have a nice day and drive safely."

Word spread in Steuben like the gypsy moth, first the cars in Weaver's driveway, then in the Town Garage and now the road block. The rumors were exotic: a SAC plane from Griffiss Air Force Base crashed, missing children, extra- terrestrial landings. Reading the Sunday Utica Observer Dispatch newspaper explained the intent, a possible homicide in their sleepy little town.

Latteiman Road was chosen as the probable site of the crime scene. It was cordoned off and patrol cars roved the lanes. The investigation took a quicker pace than was expected. Returning and concentrating in the cul-de-sac area, they found a card from a hairdresser and a rosary. The key from the Central Motel prompted a discussion between the troopers. The dialogue began, "Did you ever stay at the Central Motel when you went to the Academy for in-service? one asked . "Kind of a strange combination, rosary beads and a motel key. If it's a 'no-tell motel,' 'a hot pillow place', why pray?"

Major Charland dispatched a trooper to go to the motel,- bird dog the key, get names of people who signed in for the past six months, and didn't care if they had to embarrass some legislators, senators, assemblymen. Investigator Wassall was chosen for the task. The motel wasn't busy except during racing season, in August when Saratoga was open. It was the second trip to Albany for Troop D in less than 24 hours. Wassal confirmed the previous data, Mary Rose Turner occupied room 3 on April 23, 1973 and a guy from Rome stayed there in January. The auditor said that neither party turned their key in when they left. Jotting down some notes, asking for a copy of the register, thanking the manager for his cooperation and refusing a cup of stale coffee, Wassall called the Command Post after being patched in by Headquarters. "Got confirmation on room 3, Mary Rose Turner, Court Street, Utica, 21 April '73. I'll bring copies of the register." Roman thought the early identification of the alleged victim was a positive omen.

Investigator T. Carl welcomed the shared authority extended by Charland. They had a mutual respect for each other's qualities and worked well together. Tom Carl, having confirmed it was Mrs. Turner who had the key and the evidence found, went to Court Street, hoping he'd find Mrs. Turner there and not a next of kin notification, which he dreaded. The Jenny's answered the door and told Carl they saw Mary Rose last, two days ago, late Thursday night. They spoke of her being locked out, asking for assistance to get her coat and how she was a little snippy when they asked her where she was going so late. They deferred Carl to their tenant's brother, Bill Byrnes. They knew that, of Mrs. Turner's ten siblings, she was closest to Bill.

Bill Byrnes was a cracker- jack mechanic at a Chevrolet Dealer in Barneveld, 11 miles north of Utica. Investigator Carl met him at the garage and shared what vague information he had about her connection, key, rosary, red coat. Bill told him he reported his sister missing to the U.P.D. after she didn't answer her phone and the Jenny's hadn't seen her. Carl was a seasoned investigator with extreme tact, knowing when to be tender, when to be tough. This was a moment to be delicate. Carl asked, "What were your sister's habits, you know, who was she close to, any friends, anyone she had an affection for?" It was an elusive way to determine whether she had a male suitor who was not disclosed. Her closest brother began with a litany of tales. "He was awful to her, I mean her husband. She deserved better than him, he drove her crazy, that jerk. Tried to kill her, beat her. She gave him five great kids and he doesn't even know them. I'm sorry for feeling so bad about him but he's a son-of-a-bitch." It's SOP in homicides to consider the present, or ex-spouse, to be the primary person of interest, regardless of their relationship. Carl went to the records room of the U.P.D. and got a copy of the report Bill had furnished. It stated, "File 6: last seen at 2:30 a.m. on Thursday, reported by brother at 4:18 p.m., same date. Mary Rose Turner, eyes-blue, height 65", weight 130 pounds, hair-brown, glasses."

Carl was reluctant to ask the final question and his voice showed some hesitancy as he spoke, "Mr. Byrnes, would you care to accompany me to Oneida as we have some items we'd like you to identify." In the earliest stage of denial he retorted, "Not hers?" The investigator dodged the question as he said, "No, just some personal stuff the men picked up in Steuben. We hope and pray it isn't your sister's, but you never know."

Byrnes agreed to leave work and ride the 37 miles to Oneida to identify what was found at the turnaround. Tom Ash, a classic sleuth with a New England accent that could deceive the listener to think he was a bumpkin, met them at the door of Troop D Headquarters. After introductions he escorted Byrnes to the forensic lab. Bill was quiet as he looked around the room-photos, jars, bones, made the room look cluttered. Ash held up the retrieved exhibits and one at a time, he showed them to Bill, first the rosary. Bill's pupils enlarged as he answered to the display, "Uh-huh, that's Mary's, I'm sure. She was always religious. She felt bad about her divorce, the Church and all their sanctions. You know how that goes." Ash held up the next piece of evidence, the eye glasses and held them at the stem for a full view. "Those are Mary's too." He started rubbing his eyes, feigning a better look, but really wiping a tear away that trickled down his cheek. The next was the charred fiber but wasn't as sure about ownership as he was the beads and glasses. At this juncture, Bill asked if there was a water fountain nearby and Ash led him to the hallway and waited for his return. Bill was quiet as they went back to the lab. The final piece of evidence was the business card from the Utica School of Beauty Culture. Bill cupped the card in his hand and said, "Mary always had her hair done there."

The point of the compass was at 359 degrees-it was probably Bill's sister, Mary Rose, who was dragged to her death on Thursday. After shaking Bill's hand, Ash put his hand on his shoulder, in a consoling fashion, and said, "We'll keep in touch Mr. Byrnes, appreciate your help. Keep your chin up my friend." Bill responded, "Likewise, I will try."

Bill was somber as he rode back to Barneveld. The glimmer of hope was waning.

Positive identification of evidence, with absolute certainty, is crucial. Seems to be-I guess it is-maybe-probably, never makes the grade, scientific analysis passes the litmus test. Identifying the eyeglasses as hers was preliminary, the prescription and records of the optometrist would be verification. James Whitman of Krystal Optical wrapped it up, Mary Rose bought them in November, 1971.

The National Guard, upon mobilization, arrived in convoy at the crime scene at 9:30 a.m. Saturday April 28th. The Battalion had many combat and support personnel, Korean War veterans, Viet Nam, and some eager recruits who had finished basic training at Fort McClellan, Alabama. They were a STRAK outfit, patriotic and "Gung-Ho." They were happy to escape from the Armory on Culver Avenue, Utica, and complement the state police in the field. Some of the guardsmen were full time police officers. The mundane alternative was to watch training films or lectures in the dingy classrooms. Major Evans was enthusiastic about the opportunity for his men to get some OJT, on the job training. Roman introduced Evans to his counterpart, Major Charland, at the Command Center. Ted Wolff and Tom Carl were there also to welcome the major and thank him for his response. They briefed Evans on the drill on how they perceived their role and the protocol, if a body was discovered, invoking the law and procedure called, "Posse Comitatus." The standard for that statute is that if a guardsman locates evidence they must beckon a police officer to assist him/her. It is a long existing process dating back to the sheriff's role in the early days of our nation. They must be working in concert and the guardsman occupies the legal position of "Posse Comitatus" thus protected by the law. It usually applies in an arrest situation and it is essentially being deputized.

Wolff wanted the mandates carefully followed as he knew he may have to explain the legality at trial. The M.P.'s were well schooled in the concept and how the game must be played. Dressed in fatigues, combat boots, field jackets and helmet liners with M.P. conspicuous in white letters. They were broken down in platoons with one trooper as their guide and point man. They were there until 1630 hours, 4:30 PM. Evans promised Charland that if they came up empty they'd be back the next day and optimism was in the air.

The combination of evidence, so far, was that Mrs. Turner had met with foul play, her body disposed of and the primary suspect was driving a shiny green Chrysler with a trailer hitch, white male. Some of the troopers alluded to the possibility it was a neighbor in Steuben, without stating a name.

Investigator Bartkowiak was dispatched to Syracuse to search and secure Mrs. Turner's Nova that was under the care of Mary Ann. They were able to locate the car through Bill Byrnes and Mary Ann. The investigator went through the car like a fine comb used to screen head lice. The VIN and plate number that she gave the motel attendant, matched the car in Syracuse, UZ3197. The odometer read: 18,867 miles, seemingly high for a 56 year old divorcee who took a bus to work. The lube and oil change sticker on the door jamb reflected servicing at 15,880 miles, done in Barneveld, probably by her brother Bill. The interior was clean and uncluttered. Bartkowiak delivered, on his way home, to Tom Ash: handkerchief with a blood stain, book of matches from the Central Motel, a white pill, camera with a roll of film in it, Bufferin tablets strewn on the floor of the car. Nothing found could be classified as belonging to a male. With the families consent, the car was brought to the North Syracuse State Police Station and then towed to the Oneida Headquarters for further examination. Nothing pertinent was found.

Investigators Carl and Thomas met with Brother Bill Byrnes and Clyde Turner, Mary Rose's son, at Mrs. Turner's flat on Court Street. No one was certain that the missing relative wasn't in the house, alone and dead. It was a well kept home, dusted and waiting for a new day's event. Carl walked from the living room to the bedroom, the bathroom and then to the kitchen, masking a spooky feeling and careful not to disturb anything until they agreed what was essential. Everything seemed to fit, pictures, religious displays and a calendar with events, birthdays, anniversaries and doctors appointments, penciled in the squares. The phone was next to a comfortable chair, flanked by an end table with a reference book on top, containing pages of names, numbers and addresses. Bill and Clyde stayed in the living room.

Carl thought it indelicate to share with the family what he was focusing on a phantom lover that no one, other than Mary Rose, knew of, probably married and couldn't disclose a relationship. His suspicion was unfounded. What they didn't find was her purse. Some significant personal property was taken after receiving permission from Clyde and Bill: two photos of Mary Rose for distribution to police agencies, a blue comb with hair specimens, an extra set of car keys, some family history papers and some with disjointed writings, a list of telephone numbers, a nightgown, slippers and stockings. Knowing the State Police dog would be brought to the scene, these elements could be crucial.

Investigator Traub was commissioned with interviewing William Turner, the victim's ex-spouse. Based on the sketchy facts they had, they wanted to either eliminate or target him as a suspect. His alibi was supported as he denied seeing Mary Rose since April 10, a Wednesday night. His time card and fellow workers at General Electric had worked from midnight on the 24th until 8 a.m. on the 25th. After completing his shift he went home to Waterville, slept until late in the afternoon and went to a retirement party Thursday night. Traub noted that Turner owned a '71 white Nova.

Tracking the business card clue found at the cul-de-sac, Investigators Cerro and Arcuri were delegated to authenticate Bill Byrnes statement that Mrs. Turner was a regular customer at the School of Beauty Culture. The owner was contacted at her home since the school was closed on Saturday, and she promised to get back to them on Monday after reviewing her appointment records. Ms. Howarth kept her word and confirmed the missing woman as a regular and had two recent appointments, one for a cut on April 18th and a shampoo on the 24th, closing the relationship between the school and the victim.

Tom Carl always took that extra step in an investigation and decided he had overlooked something when he first visited the Utica Police records custodian. Greeted in the lobby by the cops on duty, they'd ask, "How's the Captain," acknowledging that Tom was a second generation cop and his father was a well respected retired Captain with the U.P.D. Captain Williams asked, "What's up Tom, second trip, must be something brewing." Tom answered, "Turner,, female type, reported by her brother as missing." Williams asked, "What's the S.P. in on it for, she's a Utica person?" Carl said," She might be the lady that we're looking for in Steuben, dragged by some pervert." He asked if there were any other missing persons in their docket.. Thumbing through his open files Williams came up with two entries: Linda and Lisa Cady, mother and daughter, missing since June 20, 1970 and Lorraine Zinicola and three sons since July 8, 1971. They were the only persons reported missing and still open.

Saturday was consumed with an intense and tiring sequence of checking, validating, sorting and organizing the Command Post and dispersing investigators for interviews. The M.P.'s were unsuccessful in recognizing anything valuable to the crime scene. They returned to the Armory anxious to be mustered on Sunday and resume their mission.

The Senior A.D.A., Ted Wolff arrived early Sunday morning, trading his dark blue suit for hunting garb. Major Evans and his charges were ready to attack the woods again. He hoped the MUTA (Multiple Unit Training Assembly} would be fruitful. By 0800 hours the field kitchen was ready with stoves blasting, trays and ranks displayed, and told the 95

Bravos (designation for the military occupational specialty of military police) that the master menu called for lasagna. The Command Post had worked out the logistical problems and functioning at full tilt.

The S.P helicopter was making passes over the searchers as they were paired up as they were the day before, one trooper per platoon. On Sunday, 11:45 a.m. a pair of guardsmen whistled and beckoned to the trooper leader, Trooper Reese, who was a few yards away. Dan Humann and Ray Spoor followed the admonition and knew the process of the "Posse Comitatus" rules. One hundred feet south of Latteiman Road, enmeshed in thick underbrush and in a heavily wooded part of the preserve, Reese responded to their waves and whistle and they agreed that the fresh dirt next to a slight convex mound was worth inspection. They were accurate. The find was 2,000 feet west of where Chaffee and Weaver saw the matted meadow and within spitting distance of where the ENCON crew gave way to the shiny green car. Reese folded his arms, placing his right hand to his chin and started to stroke it, gazing at the mound for a full minute, silently. Thinking it unusual and suspicious, he felt it best to get a second opinion. He called Sergeant P. B. Rocker for assistance. The consensus was that it might be a grave. It was.

In deference to the specialists, they knew it was time to call Tom Ash located at the Command Post two miles away. Trooper Rocker radioed to the C.P. and Ash was on his way.

Arriving with Investigator Jasek a half step behind, Tom Ash rubbed his gloved hands together as if he was ready to go to work. He circled the mound twice and then went to his knees with a small utensil, somewhat like the ones archeologists use and started to scrape away the dirt. He feared messing up the crime scene, if in fact, it was a crime scene. The onlookers wondered what was beneath the clay soil.

Realizing the process was delicate and time consuming, the guardsmen repaired to the chow line and devoured the lasagna. Even in a mess kit it was tasty. When the C.P. was alerted that a pile of soil was found, the banter and conversation increased, trusting that James Weaver wasn't delusional and the hunt was fruitful. Ted Wolff came to watch Ash's tedious task. At 6' 7" his gigantic strides left Dr. Redmond, the Oneida County Coroner, many steps behind. Dr. Redmond was called to Steuben by Major Charland. Identification is seldom pleasant

51

and often heart wrenching. The scraping soon displayed a dismembered corpse with many parts.

A cook's helper arrived at the scene and everyone except Ash declined the tray. Not intending to be disrespectful but his New England manners conditioned him to accept an invitation from a gracious host. The cook was aghast when Ash accepted a tray and the hardened examiner proceeded to consume the Italian meal, sitting astride of the mound.

Mike Jasek asked of Ash, "What have you got, oh fearless leader?" He knew Tom would have a non-direct response and knew it would be meaningful. Ash said, "In response, I'll bet it's something you have never seen before and beyond the realm of belief." Jasek asked a second question, "Male or female Tom?" Ash retorted, "Can't tell, I flunked biology." He wasn't being flippant, the remains couldn't reveal the gender.

Dr. Redmond declared the corpse dead at the scene. The Ackley Funeral Home was called and the remains were delivered to St. Elizabeth's Hospital in Utica. The M.P. Battalion left Steuben at 1630 hours. The case of murder was a few hours away from undertaking a difficult job of identifying the victim.

Chapter 8

The Autopsy

St. Elizabeth Hospital is the designated morgue for Oneida County who reimburses the hospital for its use. Isolated from the rest of the floors for obvious reasons, it is in the cellar. The identifier is room 44, ID room 43.

St. E's, as it is often referred to, has been in business since 1866 and is run by the Sisters of St. Francis. The yellow brick building sets well back from the main street in Utica, on Genesee Street.

Overlooking the lawn and the main entrance steps, stands a white statue of the Blessed Virgin Mary. The morgue is a well kept secret, as is the psychiatric ward on the third floor.

The entrance hallway into the morgue is less than glamorous, eight feet wide, tile floors, open steam pipes overhead and inconsistent colors on the concrete block walls. The autopsy room is about the size of an average living room, 16' X 20'. As one passes the gurneys you notice they are atypical with four uprights, stainless steel, allowing the attendant to place a shroud over the corpse if it happens to be wheeled through a corridor or descending on the elevator, protecting the view of a person who may feel uncomfortable.

There is a crucifix on the wall, cabinets and bones containing parts of the body that are indexed by name and date. It's an ominous scene. Ventilation isn't apparent but the cellar is air conditioned. The equipment is unusual for a hospital setting- a head brace that looks like a yoke, suction to extract blood, scales in grams and kilos, butcher blocks and a surgical saw with a rotary blade. Their uses are obvious.

The coolers are stacked, four in all, with two on each side. The handles are like those you'd see in a meat market. It's probably statutory since specimens and vital parts are stored, sometimes, for 25 years.

The assigned troopers griped about being there, even though they understood the importance of the chain of custody and to avoid an inference by a defense attorney that the body and parts were tampered with. The seriousness of having troopers as sentries is that the identification of the body was going to be, whether it is Mary Rose Turner, predicated on the disfigurement and butchering.

One of the guards carped about the duty and said, "Who's going to steal her? She's in a fridge, padlocked from the outside and in the cellar of a secured hospital. What a waste of manpower." Watching over a truncated body wasn't their notion of action. They may have developed discomfort as they considered it could be their mother or grandmother.

Trooper Sam Jess was the first link in the chain of custody. Watching but not touching the deceased, he escorted what little remains were left of Mrs. Turner. He rode shotgun in the back of the hearse on the way to St. E's. He was close to his thirteenth year on the troop and never felt easy around dead people. It was a long 30 minute ride for Sam from Steuben. Parking in the emergency room entrance, Jess helped remove the remains on to a gurney. He was happy to be relieved at 4:30 and went home. Someone said he smelled like decayed flesh. He accompanied the procession from the hearse to the elevator and reluctantly shed his raincoat.

Trooper Bergstrom was waiting for the cortege. He was on C line, 3 to 11 and his eight years as a cop didn't include a tour at a morgue. He was passed the orders of the day from his predecessor and was told, "Stand in the hallway, don't allow anyone except medical personnel in or out. The body is in the cooler, or should be." Bergstrom was in a better mood than Jess and had dinner with his family before his shift.

Five days after he had last spoken to his sister, Bill Byrnes arrived at the information desk. His nephew, Clyde was with him. It was about 5:30 p.m. Bill was ten years younger than Mary Rose and had the deepest regard for his older sister. He was later than he had promised to be but had forgotten to turn his watch ahead. .He thought he'd be able to handle his emotions better than he did. Bergstrom was summoned to greet the relatives and bring them to the morgue. If he had a choice he'd rather be under a dentist's drill. He opened the door to the morgue and like an usher in a concert hall, he extended his arm allowing entrance to a scene he knew was going to be jittery.

Dr. Redmond had followed the hearse in his car and met the pair as they entered. Used to being amid tragedies, he gracefully said, "Hi, I'm Dr. Redmond, Coroner." Neither shared their name and he continued, "What you are going to see is not pleasant. I can't say it any easier, she's a mess, there isn't much left of her, poor thing. She's been dragged and dismembered and it may be hard to----identify her. Do your best and I'll be right here." Trooper Bergstrom was listening outside the door, grateful he didn't have to break the news.

The interim vault was purposely located in a remote location, with no identification. It's next to the cafeteria and functionally close to the refrigeration supply. Its location was placed intentionally by the architect to be distanced from traffic. The sentry wondered whether her murderer would be caught and testifying at a trial twenty months later, never entered his mind. Just before Christmas of 1974, Bergstrom was summoned by the prosecution to close any doors that may smack of corpse tampering, destruction of evidence and to remove any hint of a rupture in the chain of custody. He had testified often during his career and was schooled by Ted Wolff as he went over the events, date, time and place. His response to the direct examination was calm, direct and poised. He was surprised when Defense Attorney Pawlinga asked if he had a notebook with him and whether the body was placed on a surgical table. He also asked if she was on her back or on her front, face down. The Q and A follows:

> Q: I noticed every time he (Wolff) asked you a question,
>   you turned your head to the jury? Where did you
>   learn that?
> A: They taught us that at the Academy.
> Q: They taught you to look at the jury, is that true?
> A: Yes sir!

A subtle question, an honest response and a short primer on the preparation of testimony, courtesy of the New York State Police.

Dr. Redmond had put in a full day. He was at Steuben most of the afternoon and then to the morgue. It was a chore to finesse the relatives into thinking his description was less than gross.

Handling the evidence with caution and trying to avoid contamination, Dr. Redmond, for identification purposes, pointed to the ear, locks of hair, the nape of the neck and finally the other detached ear. Grasping for more graphic parts to observe and avoid an error, Bill Byrnes asked a moot question, "Could we see her nose, Doctor?" "Sorry Mr. Byrnes, I wish I could, there is no nose, there is no face." Without concluding, this is my aunt, that's my sister, they were convinced that it was Mary Rose. In a final gesture to remove all doubt, Clyde asked to see her leg. It had been amputated and the Coroner placed it on the table. "That's hers" he gasped.

In the early stages of the trial and as Wolff tried to prove that it was Mary Rose who was killed, Bill Byrnes responded to the direct examination after looking at the 8 X 10 glossy:

> Q: OK. I show you peoples exhibit 18 and I ask you if
>   that shows the area that you saw in the hospital?
> A: God forgive him.
> Q: In other words, the ear and the hair?
> A: Yes, that's the back of her neck. She had good skin
>   for a woman 56.

It was an emotional moment for Mr. Byrnes. He looked away from the exhibit and tried to make eye contact with the man who didn't blink, and iterated, "God forgive him" in a quaking voice. The A.D.A. didn't coax him to say that, an explosive expletive that got into the record and wasn't objected to.

Fast forward to the trial testimony, as the defense attorney ventured into a crucible of guilt deflection and direct the accusation of murder on William Turner, her ex-spouse. During Mr. Byrnes cross by Pawlinga, he testified the Mary Rose's husband tried to kill her two or three times by trying to drown her and was choking her on one occasion, until the kids stopped him. The arrow of guilt was deflected by Mr. Byrnes by a sorrowful statement that his sister tried to commit suicide, working three jobs and worried about a gall bladder operation. He added, she was confined to Denton Hall at Utica Psychiatric Center for six months. He emoted a tragic side of his sister's life, plagued with disappointments, distrust and infidelity. Her bizarre association with Hatch was the final straw of a dreadful life.

New York State laws do not require that a coroner has to be a doctor. The coroner is an elected court officer, often an embalmer, funeral director, or an ordinary citizen with no particular skills. They pronounce people dead, may request an inquest. The autopsy is performed by a licensed pathologist supporting the probable cause or causes of death. Dr. Redmond wasn't a pathologist, Dr. Legrand Thomas was. The ritual began after the relatives had left. Photographs were taken, black and white to show bleeding and bruises and a 16 mm camera taped the method and movements of the surgeon. Dr. Thomas dictated into a tape recorder. His diagnosis was: "A dismembered body, marked mutilation, secondary to dragging, loss of vital organs, lower and upper extremities received separately. Half of the head is absent, the facial portion. The brain is absent. The entire body is covered with gravel. No teeth present. The jaw is missing. There is a rope mark about the neck ½ inch in width and comes to a V in the middle of the back of the neck. The upper extremities are absent. The lower 2/3 or the lower arm, hand, including the fingers are absent. The knee, lower leg ankle and foot are absent. Gross diagnosis: Mutilated torso of body. My verdict is death by strangulation and suffocation. Homicide."

It was the opinion of Tom Ash that the fingers were butchered to avoid identification through prints. They were never found. Dr. Thomas would be under oath for six days at the trial. Ms. Howarth would identify the hair as being similar to the razor cut Mrs. Turner had as a routine, Ralph Marcucio of the state police Lab would be on the stand for four days. They would be the last people's witnesses before the prosecution rested. Their testimony will be detailed in the trial chapter. It was a grotesque feature of the trial that the only components to identify the corpse would be strands of hair, not fingerprints or teeth.

Chapter 9

Search Warrants

"The right of the people to be secure in their persons, papers and effects, against unreasonable searches and seizure, shall not be violated---." There are 54 words in the fourth amendment to the Constitution, all contained in one paragraph. Countless arguments, testimony, briefs and appeals have been delivered before the courts since the enactment in 1782. The judiciary has required a strictness when an application has been presented and the right and expectation of privacy have been sacred, jealously protected and are comfortable and demanding safeguards.

There are many technical requirements and restrictive rules attached to a request for a search warrant. Jurisdiction, affidavits, detailed description of the premises to be entered, the person or persons residing or present in the home or business and the appearance and swearing of the applicant before the magistrate. In New York State the warrant may only be issued by a superior court judge, county or supreme court magistrate. The judge must be unequivocally convinced of the presented facts, based on probable cause, not reasonable suspicion of the knowledge of the applicant. The petitioner must have more than subjective opinions. It is a delicate request.

If the warrant is approved and issued, the police officer must execute it within 10 days and in most instances, served between 6:00 a.m. and 9:00 p.m. unless it has been proven that the persons will not be present during those hours. Another modifier is to permit a "No knock warrant" if the police officer argues that an announcement would place lives in danger. Both must be supported by factual data.

The law further states that if property is removed, held or examined as evidentiary proof, a receipt must be tendered to the owner or occupant. The issuing magistrate must also have a copy of the inventory seized. If a copy has not been left with the owner/occupant, the court must convey it. The criteria is stringent.

Attorney Wolff's extensive background, attention to detail and comprehensive work ethic, made him appreciative of the insistence of the amendment. Rarely, if ever, did he have evidence suppressed after a warrant was issued, based on quirks or improper applications. He was a student of the law, kept abreast of the most recent appellate decisions and had an insight as to any peculiarities judge's may have. Gallagher and Carl were equally adept at the skills required for obtaining a search warrant.

The investigators had more than an inkling that Hatch had been living with his sister and her husband in their trailer on Soule Road. The property to be examined and possibly seized was outlined carefully in the request: digging equipment, knives (butcher and hunting), hatchets, axes, rope and fibers, clothing, shoes (or other footwear), binoculars, a 1966 green Plymouth automobile, plate number 319UKW and a green Plymouth automobile, plate number 072OUT. The request asked the court for permission to search the trailer, the outbuildings and land, owned and occupied by the Pulcini's and Bernard P. Hatch. As the source of Gallagher's information and basis of belief, he supported it by his own personal investigation, the members of the New York State Police and an addendum, the affidavit taken from Stephen Earl.

The application was proffered before Arthur Darrigrand, an Oneida County Court Judge. He had followed the usual pattern by serving as the District Attorney and then being elected as a County Court Judge. He was a mild mannered person, held in high esteem by the Bar, consistent in his decisions, stickler for detail and a keen observer of personalities. The reaction of both defendants and their attorneys was one of equity and justice when they appeared before him. As a prosecutor, he helped to draft numerous applications for search warrants and had an instinct whether the probable cause recited was weak or strong.

The D.A.'s office called the court clerk to alert the judge that an application was to be submitted and a request for an appointment to review the merits of the warrant. Time was of the essence as they wanted to get the belongings before Hatch disposed of them. Gallagher, Carl and Wolff entered the judge's chambers a few minutes before the designated appointment time. Offering them a seat and finishing the task that was on hand, he said, "What's on your minds, gentlemen?" Wolff handed him the documents and the anxious trio watched as he scrutinized the papers. After a 10 minute interlude, Judge Darrigrand leaned back in his chair and said, "This is quite a laundry list you have here, gentlemen. Sounds like you're going to invade Attila the Hun's castle." The applicants looked at each other and smirked. They realized he wasn't taking this as a frivolous warrant for a pornography or gambling bust and that this was a serious matter.

Gallagher stood up and tacked on the details of uncovering the corpse from the shallow grave and how pivotal it was to obtain the evidence. He said, "Your honor, you wouldn't believe the condition of the body, it was the most gross thing I've witnessed in my career and I thought I had seen it all." He continued with his delivery describing in detail the dismemberment, the absence of any identification other than hair and ear lobes, lack of fingerprints, teeth and the drag marks for nine and one half miles.

It was time for the magistrate to ask some burning questions. "Now Pulcini and his wife. Are they suspects? Are they in on this or are you targeting Hatch as your primary and sole suspect?" Tom Carl entered into the discussion when he said, "Your honor, we want Hatch. He's been around before. You may recall he was acquitted a few years ago when he raped a lady who didn't know the last names of her children and took the stand looking like a street walker. Judge McCarthy presided over a trial in Herkimer County when he was convicted of rape and kidnapping while he was on leave from the Marine Corps. He's bad people judge!"

Darrigrand was a little uncomfortable with the intrusion into Pulcini's home and the fact that Hatch was a tenant or a guest, when he asked, "Are you limiting, restricting your search to the bedroom Hatch is staying in, if in fact he has his own bedroom in a trailer, or are you broad-brushing it to include all the bedrooms, even the one the Pulcini's stay in?" Wolff gave Gallagher a slight poke indicating he thought Tom could handle the answer. "Your honor, we hope that we will discover all necessary evidence in Hatch's room and his cars. We'll be poking around the premises, sheds and grounds. We've had the premises under constant surveillance since last Thursday and we're convinced he has in his possession what we need for an arrest. Our information is that there are 3 bedrooms." The judge seemed satisfied with the response.

The judge raised his eyes in a pensive manner, stroked his chin and proceeded. "I know I don't have to remind you about the inventory routine and protocol that the statute demands, but I will. Since you've shot-gunned this warrant, lots of tools and such, make sure you detail all of the items you're seizing and that the list must be left with the owner, Pulcini. Oh yes, one more thing: if something is serialized, I want the number."

Gallagher had a gut feeling that the judge was close to giving them a thumbs up and was ready to approve their request. "Your honor, we'll be diligent, itemizing everything we grab, I mean seize, and will be scrupulous in compliance with the statute. The media hooked onto this case earlier than we had hoped and wanted them to. They're up in Steuben and been there since Saturday when the National Guard showed up and they've sensationalized this whole thing. We're sure Hatch reads the paper and watches TV and this massive manhunt would alert Hatch and maybe destroy the evidence we're looking for. To be honest with you, we may be too late, he may have already dumped what we need."

Darrigrand was satisfied that the paper work was in order and within the confines of the law and signed the warrant. Wolff gave the investigators a smile, acknowledging success. The judge wished them luck and with a degree of certainty said, "See you again, gentlemen, best of luck."

Knowing that the execution had to be errorless and thorough, Gallagher assigned investigators Ash, Jasek, Gildersleeve and Arcuri, plus a half dozen uniformed troopers to accompany him to the trailer. It was five days after Weaver sighted the dragging, two days following the discovery of the corpse. They were all familiar with Hatch's propensities but unsure what his most dangerous act could be. The article in the May 1 edition of the Utica Observer Dispatch said, "Police reportedly were looking for a greenish-blue car about four years old." Gallagher was fearful the article may have provoked their suspect to either hide or destroy the car.

At precisely 4:00 p.m., May 2, 1973, the cavalcade of state police sedans arrived on Soule Road in Steuben. Some were parked in the driveway to prevent an escape, others were on the shoulders of the road in front of the trailer. Anticipating that cars may be impounded

they alerted the Oriskany Garage in Utica to be on call, in the event they needed a flat-bed to haul the evidence to Troop D Headquarters.

As the armed troopers dispersed throughout the property to prevent escape or destroying evidence, Gallagher rapped on the front door and was met by the occupants, John and Victoria Pulcini and Hatch's mother, Florence. Cassandra, Hatch's 13 year old daughter stood terrorized in the living room. Hatch wasn't there and had a scheduled meeting with his parole officer, Robert Wozna, that afternoon.

As Gallagher announced his obvious presence, handed the warrant to the owner, who said, surprised, "What the hell is this?" Gallagher answered, "It's a homicide investigation Mr. Pulcini and the court has authorized our presence. Here, read it." Mrs. Hatch blurted, "We've got our rights John, tell him that." Gallagher ignored her reaction. "This won't take long if you cooperate. Please remain in one spot as we go through the trailer. Now, which bedroom does Mr. Hatch occupy, Mr. Pulcini?" "To the rear, on the right," he answered. Cassandra clung to her grandmother as the search began. The four occupants hovered together, mumbling to themselves as dresser drawers were opened and carpets were pulled up.

Captain Griffin asked Pulcini if he would answer some questions as the troopers scoured for meaningful evidence. The trailer was cluttered and there seemed to be an abundance of furniture for such a small place. The bulky troopers constricted it also. His opening question was, "Mr. Pulcini, where was your brother-in-law, Bernard Hatch, last Thursday, April 26, 1973?" It wouldn't be interpreted as a custodial interrogation, merely the questioning of a witness, so the Miranda warning didn't have to be recited. The response was vague and cautious, "He was around, got out of work, yeah, he was around." The captain started to zone in on Hatch's activities on Thursday morning and asked, "What time did he get out of work?"

Pulcini balked at the question, but asked for a window, when he said, "What time did this murder take place?" Griffin, appearing to be cooperative and responsive, he said, "We're sorry sir, we really don't know. In fact, Mr. Pulcini, we aren't sure it is, or was, a murder." A classic response from a trained professional. Pulcini chose to exonerate Hatch, when he declared, "My brother-in-law wouldn't kill anyone, no he wouldn't!"

May 2nd wasn't Pulcini's first encounter with the troopers. Three days before, Troopers Cheseboro, Weyland-Smith and Malecki were assigned the dubious task of digging through a pile of trash placed on the side of the road in front of the trailer for a pick up. It was about 9:30 a.m. when they arrived and started to rummage through the garbage. In a few minutes, Pulcini strode aggressively towards the group, in a challenging mood. "Do you have a search warrant to paw through that stuff? If not, get lost." Trooper Cheseboro dodged the question and chose to defuse the inquiry by taking the offense when he said, "You're in violation of the town ordinance, let me see some identification." He had done his research and was aware of the Supreme Court decision, California v Greenwood. In that case, Byron White wrote the majority decision when he said, "It is common knowledge that plastic garbage bags left on the side of the street are readily accessible to animals, children, scavengers, snoops and other members of the public." Although never mentioning police agencies, the court interpreted the words "Other members of the public" to include law enforcement.

The background of the case extending the authority to search trash, was derived from the Laguna California Police Department seizing a plastic bag of trash without a warrant. Billy Greenwood's attorney would argue, in the appeal, that the search was unconstitutional and violated the protection of the fourth amendment. Traces of narcotics were found in the trash and that became the probable cause to have a search warrant issued for his home and a discovery of cocaine and hashish. As a practical matter, the majority opinion said that once a person relinquishes control of trash by setting it outside the home for disposal, the right and expectation of privacy ceases and the property becomes public and unrestricted. Pulcini would have agreed with the dissenters on the court, Brennan and Marshall, who said it was unreasonable.

Relaxing after the discussion and producing his driver's license, Pulcini asked, "What's going on here, why is there a black trooper's car always parked up the road? Every place I go I'm followed. Yesterday I was stopped for nothing on route 365 by a trooper." The discussion ended with Pulcini agreeing to comply with the ordinance. The troopers caught a glimpse of a white male standing in the window of the trailer watching the meeting. The figure matched the description of Hatch. Cheseboro also noted that there were three snow tires leaning against a small fence near the driveway along with two cars and a pick-up with summer tires on all three vehicles.

Inside the trailer, the troopers paired off, continuing their inspection for hard evidence. Gallagher approached Florence Hatch, and in a cordial manner asked, "Tell us about Bernard's activities on Thursday the 27th, short of a week ago." Her crisp reply was, " I don't have to talk to state police!" Undaunted he approached Cassandra, an eighth grader who was street wise and devoted to her dad despite being a divorced father and a tour in prison. Before he could voice the words, Cassandra's grandmother stepped between the investigator and the child and warned, "She's not answering your questions!"

After the cars were identified, the flat-bed was summoned. Of the two identified in the warrant, only one was present, the '66 Plymouth sedan. The '70 Dodge, registered in the name of Florence Hatch, was later found on the premises of a dealer in Utica. Both were transported to Oneida to be scrutinized by the forensic investigators.

Within an hour after the search began, Hatch traipsed through the front door, composed and appearing compliant, but not surprised. Captain Griffin ushered him to his bedroom at the far end of the trailer and was read his rights from a card the captain held in his hand. "Mr. Hatch, you have the right to remain silent, need make no statement unless you desire to do so, any statement you may make could be and will be used against you at the time of trial. You are entitled to be represented by an attorney at that time and all future stages of the proceedings, and if you can't afford an attorney, one will be provided at no cost. Do you understand these rights?"

After a long silence, Hatch replied, "Yes, I do." Investigator D. J. Arcuri stood in the doorway of the bedroom, acting as a sentry and a witness to the Miranda warning. Griffin then broached Hatch's activities on Thursday morning, April 26. Hatch answered, "I worked at the gas station until 7:30 in the morning, came to the trailer and got here about 9:00 a.m." "Mr. Hatch, did you remain at the trailer after

9:00 a.m.?" Hatch snapped back, "If you want to know anymore, see my lawyer!" After a long interval, Hatch said, "You guys have been on my back for years." Griffin, knowing the interrogation was aborted couldn't resist a parting shot when he said, "Mr. Hatch, you're only paranoid if no one is out to get you!" Hatch stood mute.

At this juncture the suspect was asked to strip completely. Griffin and Arcuri scanned his thick, muscular build. They later discussed the cleanliness of his hands, manicured finger nails and that they didn't fit with his job as an auto mechanic. They noted there were no scratch marks, bruises or cuts. He was told to get dressed with no further dialogue. They didn't obtain anything incriminating during the strip search. They'd be satisfied with the physical evidence gathered from the trailer and property.

The inventory of seized property displayed 36 individual items removed, carefully tagged and bagged. The most vital were: camera, negatives, Timex watch with a cracked crystal, sales slips, letters, telephone numbers, six knives, newspaper clippings about the Turner homicide, miscellaneous men's clothing, shoes, boots, shovel, stained cloth, four snow tires and a glove. The '66 Plymouth was inventoried at Troop D Headquarters.

As darkness started to fall, Gallagher signed the inventory that was removed, carefully handed it to Pulcini and bid a farewell. There was only one disparity between what Gallagher gave to Pulcini and what he delivered to the court. It was "One white glove and one newspaper with clipping from trash," left with the trailer owner and the copy delivered to the court was, "One right glove and one newspaper with portions cut out." After scanning the inventory, Judge Darrigrand released the evidence to the investigators for further examination by the State Police Laboratory in Albany. Hairs recovered from the tan leather shoes were shipped to the Treasury Department Lab in Washington, D.C. for neutron examination.

Intelligence information told the State Police that Hatch spent Thursday night with his mother as she tended to the Hinman home in Deansboro, 14 miles southwest of Utica and 32 miles from Steuben. An interview with Cassandra revealed her recollection as spending Thursday night in Forestport with her father.

Two weeks after the trailer search, Investigator Frank Peo, applied for a second search warrant naming and identifying the Hinman home in Deansboro. The supporting affidavit described the investigator's attempts at interviewing Hatch's mother failed and the property was characterized as, "A ranch style home located north of the village on State Route 12B." His surveillance disclosed that 4 tires were observed in the two stall attached garage as, "Two snow tires with good tread remaining and two summer tires which appear to be wide ovals with good tread remaining." The tires were seen on the outside wall of the garage as you look in from the driveway through the windows of the garage door. The warrant was accepted and signed by Judge John Walsh. On Monday May 15, 1973, Peo, Gallagher and Senior Investigator Conley, served the warrant on Florence Hatch. In addition, they gathered a length of rope, a hunting knife, two pieces of red cloth two Goodyear poly-glass belted tires, 660X15. The significance of the second search was an attempt to validate and reinforce the perception of the witnesses, Earl and Winters, who would later testify that the passing Plymouth on Latteiman Road during their lunch hour had wide ovals. The assembly of the circumstantial evidence was beginning to take form.

Chapter 10

The Trial

The prosecutor and the defense had thirteen months to prepare the case for trial. Oneida County has the rare distinction of having two county seats, Utica and Rome. In addition to the many agencies that have duplication, there are two courtrooms and therefore two calendars. The trial of the People v Bernard P. Hatch began in Rome and then continued in Utica.

Hatch was confined to the Oneida County Jail in Oriskany, half way between the two cities and held without bail after indictment. Hatch was considered a high risk since he was charged with murder in the 2nd degree. In 1975 the maximum sentence was 25 years to life as the death penalty was removed from the Criminal Procedure Law.

On November 6, 1975, jury selection began. The commissioner of jurors sent letters to 600 potential jurors in Oneida County. The original group of 200 received summonses to report for potential selection. The criminal justice system applies the word Talisman, a carry over from English Common Law, identifying jurors. The process is called Voir Dire, translated meaning "To speak the truth."

Defense Attorney Pawlinga argued that the jurors should be questioned outside the hearing of others and were challenged in the judge's chambers. Pawlinga was fearful that the pre-trial publicity would preclude the defendant from getting a fair trial and felt he would be prejudiced by the newspaper articles. Judge Walsh agreed and the questioning was closed with only the two attorneys, stenographer and bailiff present.

Of the original group, two weeks later, 150 were excused for a variety of reasons, health, jobs, family demands and lack of objectivity. Judge Walsh allowed the press to be in chambers. The trial was expected to last two months, based on the number of witnesses listed to testify. The estimate was 60 days short of reality. A motion was made by Pawlinga for a change of venue since he felt a local jury would not be open and objective, based on the media reporting. He reserved decision but kept an open mind when he ruled that if an unbiased jury cannot be chosen, then he would rule in favor of a change in venue, but not before.

It was an arduous task and it was a week before the first juror was acceptable to both parties. The attorneys were allowed 20 peremptory challenges, which meant they didn't have to declare a reason for excusing the party. It could be as vague as a hunch, a sense that they didn't fit the profile they were looking for. There was no limit on the number of challenges for cause but the judge had to rule on the outcome. Cause must be obvious: related to someone in law enforcement, friend or acquaintance of a potential witness, knew the attorneys or any form of relativity that wouldn't allow them to make an unbiased decision as to guilt or innocence.

On November 20, 1975, there were 400 names drawn and only three jurors agreed upon. It was just short of a month before a panel was chosen at long last, twelve plus four alternates, consisting of thirteen males and three females. Pawlinga was descriptive when he later called it "A Blue Ribbon Jury." Ted Wolff used up his twenty peremptory challenges, Steve Pawlinga used ten. They both seemed satisfied on the assortment of jurors.

The process and sequence seems fair as the prosecution opens first and the prosecution closes last. Neither side would have an advantage. The trial began on December 8, 1975 after being moved to the trial calendar in Utica. from Rome.

Sitting next to the A.D.A was Tom Carl, assigned by Major Charland for the duration of the trial and excused from any other duties as an investigator. Steve Pawlinga was not an assigned counsel and was paid by the Hatch family for his representation.

The opening statements consisting of an admonishment by the lawyers to be open and attentive, rely on their background and education, depend on their instinct as to whether the witnesses are truthful and make a decision based on the preponderance of evidence submitted. The stenographer clocked the opening statements as eighteen minutes for the prosecutor and eighteen for the defense. Wolff reviewed the evidence to be presented, identification of the victim through her rosary, eye glasses, motel key, wedding band and the cause of death by the pathologist, strangulation. Pawlinga reminded them of the doctrine, "Presumption of innocence and the burden of proof necessary for conviction." He further stated that Mary Rose Turner may have died from a heart attack before her body was dismembered. In addition he alluded to the proposition that the law enforcement agencies have tried to implicate his client in every murder in Oneida County.

Prosecutor Wolff carefully created a sequence of witnesses. His yellow evidence pad outlined his presentation: prior to disappearance-after disappearance, before discovery of the body and after discovery to the present time, the trial. This technique was easy for the jury to follow as he wove a story with precision and reasoning. He would hurdle one piece of evidence at a time.

He knew that the first obstacle to overcome was that the body that was found was that of Mary Rose Turner. The identification was not scientific but simply by observation. Her son would be the main witness, Clyde Turner. The coroner and pathologist couldn't precisely identify the body as that of Mary Rose Turner. He testified that he went to the morgue and that his mother "Didn't have a face."

He further stated that the only means of identification was through the flat ear lobes caused by wearing earrings. Pawlinga under cross asked Clyde, "This could very well be someone else because you were looking at only the ears and the hairline, couldn't it?" Clyde's answer was assertive and concise as he said, "No-no-no!" His statements ended and Mrs. Turner's daughter Mary Ann took the stand. She was assertive as she connected the recovered items: lipsticks, cameo ring, wedding band, a mother's ring with four stones and a space where a stone was missing, belonging to her mother. Her identity as the victim was completed with certainty.

The next snag to overcome was to place Mrs. Turner at or near the gas station the morning of her disappearance. Corelli, Secor and Cable, the trio that saw Mrs. Turner wandering on the apron of the station, were the next witnesses. They all agreed that the woman who was in the photograph displayed by the prosecutor was the same person they saw the morning of her disappearance. Wolff was able to support the placement of Mary Rose and his next step was to put Hatch at the same location at the same time. Russell Snyder and Brian Matthews, employees of Bohling, swore that Hatch had worked the morning shift, 11 at night to 7 in the morning.

James Weaver's declaration was next on Wolff's lineup. He was steadfast and unswerving as he spoke of his sighting of the dragging, his hunt with Trooper Chaffee and his trip to Troop D Headquarters.

The defense attorney didn't ask any clarification of Weaver's delivery.

Twenty four witnesses followed in sequence, mostly state police, and investigators. The ENCON group added their viewing of a car near the site of the grave at noon time on Thursday. Dr. Redmond gave his coroners diagnosis and findings. The final difficulty for the prosecution was to tie the knot through the evidence that was available. Dr. Thomas was to take the stand for three days, Tom Ash and Mike Jasek for an equal amount of testimony.

It was the prosecutor's job to remove any hesitancy in the jurors minds and to prove conclusively and with absolute certainty that Bernard P. Hatch had murdered Mary Rose Turner without a declaration that there was a motive. Only Hatch knows what his purpose was.

Ted Wolff was mildly optimistic that he'd get a conviction but was concerned about what he felt were stumbling blocks. He relied on three vital witnesses: Ms. Howarth, Ralph Marcuccio and Joseph Nowak. He would have included the defendant if he had known that the defense attorney was going to put him on the stand. The foundation of the trial was to prove, beyond a reasonable doubt that the victim, Mrs. Turner, was in fact the person that was killed. The onus was on Ms. Howarth to make the determination through hairs. Another impediment would be the evidence that joined Hatch and his property to Mary Rose. That would be the duty of the state police chemist, Marcuccio. Joseph Nowak's credibility was an obstacle, based on his record. The testimony of the three would be crucial and had Wolff's highest priority.

Dorothy Howarth didn't require any coaching or tutoring on the art of testimony. She was a feisty, self-assured person who had savvy and wouldn't be intimidated. It was February 11 when she took the stand and Ted began his direct as he opened with the history of her vocation-a professional director at a beauty school for 26 years. She wasn't a novice but a professional. Carefully laying a strong foundation he proceeded:

Do you recall when the last time you saw Mrs. Turner prior to the 26th of April?

The morning of the 24th, on a Tuesday at about a quarter to ten.

Do you know what she had done at the time?

Yes. She had a shampoo and set.

During the period that Mary Rose Turner was using your establishment, did she also have her hair cut there?

Many times.

Do you remember the last time she had her hair cut prior to the 26th of April, 1973?

The Wednesday before that. I think it was the eighteenth.

Do you recall what type of hair she had?

It was very short. The hair was cut two, three, four inches all over her head.

How was it cut?

Short for a permanent that she was going to get the following Friday

What was used to cut the hair?

A razor.

Ted had made his point and rested. The defense attorney, almost instantly, assumed the offensive, realizing the testifier was the primary identifier of who belonged to the hair that the pathologist found.

So I understand you're the director of the Utica School of Beauty Culture?

Yes I am. I have my sister, Margie Howarth and myself who own the school.

I didn't ask you that.

Well you asked me if I was the director. Yes.

Have you previously given any written statements to the District Attorney or to the state police as to what you are testifying here today?

(Mr. Wolff) She testified before the Grand Jury.

You testified before the Grand Jury?

Yes I did. That was the first time.

Did you misunderstand what I had asked you before?

71

Yes I did.

(Mr. Wolff) Let the record show that I have given Mr. Pawlinga a copy of the Grand Jury minutes of this witness.

Ms. Howarth didn't weave or bob, she didn't even clinch with the defense attorney as the cross examination continued.

Mary Rose Turner was a patron of your establishment for about five years prior to the time you testified before the Grand Jury, is that true?

Five, six, seven, eight years. Maybe longer.

How about fifteen?

No. Not that long.

I show you page two and a question was asked of you. Do you remember the question was, "For how long a period of time, approximately?" And your answer was for five years, do you remember?

I checked and it was longer.

Were you in the Army?

No, but I'm a good director.

That's what I wanted to know.

I am known as the best in New York State. I do know about hair

Her testimony continued as she spoke of the mixture of colors in the hair and the texture. She remained unwavering. The next encounter displayed her emotions.

Did you make any tests to determine whether or not her hair or her scalp might be allergic to the shampoo? Do you have any idea what the chemical components of the shampoo were?

I am sure that I never lied

Of course you didn't, but you testified before the Grand Jury and you told them that with regard to the color, texture and so forth, it was brown and grey.

There is no question that she had some grey hair. The shampoo is the purest on the market

I will look that up

That's right, you do that.

Pawlinga was giving it his best shot but he kept missing the target as his slope became more slippery.

I take it you basically conduct a beauty salon

A beauty school

I'm sorry. Beauty School?

Yes

Have you ever looked in any microscope in your life?

Yes, all the time

When?

All the time. I have them in school

You have microscopes in school?

Yes

Ms. Howarth wasn't qualified as an expert witness before her testimony began, her statements were delivered with restrictions that she was a person who knew Mary Rose, worked on her hair for years, was a teacher and administrator. She couldn't swear that the hair recovered was that of the victim, that would be a chemist's job. She was qualified to make the statement, "I know they were human hairs, that's all." The question of whether hair continues to grow after death was presented by the cross examiner as the banter continued.

Let's say a person immediately dies, does the hair continue to grow?

Your hair will not continue to grow because when you're embalmed the blood is taken out of your body.

Do you want to bet on that?

Years ago, before they embalmed people, hair grew and nails grew.

Do you have any proof of that?

I don't know

Interviews with the jurors expressed a strong feeling of acceptance and support of the witness. They said her words were solid, practical and understandable. They accepted the premise that her means of identification would compare to today's DNA.

Four days of sworn testimony by Ralph Marcuccio followed Ms. Howarth. He was quickly accepted by the court and Mr. Pawlinga as an expert in his field as he answered to Wolff's question, "Mr. Marcuccio, where are you employed?" "I am a chemist at the New York State Lab in Albany."

Ted Wolff would hand the witness "People's Exhibits" and ask if he recalled seeing them before and what the examination revealed. In a sequence Ted walked him through the variety of items used to convince the jury that the circumstantial evidence he'd attest to was unassailable and that Hatch had murdered Mrs. Turner. He began with the rope recovered from the search of the car and the trailer.

Mr. Marcuccio, I show you People's Exhibit 25 and ask you if you recall seeing that exhibit before?

Yes. At the State Police Laboratory on April 28, 1973

Okay. That was previously identified as a piece of rope that was found on Potato Hill Road by Trooper Chaffee and Mr. Weaver on the afternoon of the 26th or early evening of the 27th. Did you make some tests with regard to that piece of rope?

Yes. I conducted a physical examination of the rope and also checked the rope for bloodstains.

Would you tell us what the physical examination revealed?

The stains were positive for blood. I then conducted a test to determine if the blood was human. In this particular case, the blood was identified as human.

Wolff then walked the chemist through more exhibits: rope from the field, rope at the intersection of Potato Hill and Latteiman roads. He compared the findings and said they were the same in both instances. The next frame of reference used to tighten the loop was the pieces of red cloth, presumably from the coat Mrs. Turner retrieved when she asked the Jenny's to open her door.

I show you People's Exhibit 14 that has been identified as a piece of red cloth, possibly part of a coat, found in the turnaround area in the Town of Steuben. Would you tell us what test, if any, you made of the material, and, also, what examination was made of it?

The material consisted of burned and charred cloth material. The material was pink-colored and the cloth was composed of pink-colored wool fibers and reddish colored acetate fibers.

Wolff then progressed to People's exhibit 15, two pieces of rope found six feet from a logging road. The professional iterated his prior findings, comparing them with the others under a microscope and found them to be the same as the others. Advancing to the shovel that was found in the search of the shed, the technician found pink-colored wool fiber that were identical to those found earlier. The prosecutor then moved to what he referred to as a "Vacuum Sweep" from Hatch's Plymouth Satellite. Marcuccio described his analysis and said, "There was a quantity of soil, leaves, paper and brown-colored polyester, orange-colored wool, red-colored acetate and pink-colored wool fiber also found." When asked if they were compared with the other fibers, he said they were the same.

Pressing on with his microscopic findings the witness corroborated the findings of Ms. Howarth during her sworn statements. He said, " I conducted a microscopic examination of a quantity of hair that was two to three inches in length. It had light to medium brown-colored hair and was fine texture. Also, several of the hair tips were razor cut." His next statement was that he compared the hair with the deceased's hair and that they were similar.

Furthering the connection he then discussed his analysis of the knife and sheath owned by Hatch, found in the dresser drawer during the search. Two hairs were recovered and were microscopically similar to the hair of the deceased. Despite being the second month of sitting and hearing testimony, the jury remained riveted to the chemist's laundry list of similarities. The closer was when Ted ventured to a piece of evidence closer than the prior exhibits, Hatch's shoes. He found blood spots and hair.

Pawlinga had an uphill battle during the cross examination. He greeted the witness in a courteous manner and said, "Good morning Mr. Marcuccio." He then questioned the tired technique of raising the authenticity of the notes, original or copies. The governmental examinations and whether he had responses from them were explored. He then wanted to know why the witness addressed the jury and not the defense lawyer as he answered him. "Did you learn to do that in some school?" he asked. It was a conditioned reflex that was a standing procedure used by the state police. His response was, "I believe what I have to say is important for the jury to hear." As if he had the ability to determine whether a witness was lying or being truthful, the defense attorney said he wanted to see his eyeballs and to see the dilation of the eyes. The next question, that received a no answer, was whether the state police Lab received the neutron analysis from the F.B.I. Marcuccio ended his testimony by stating that he had no personal knowledge that the body found was that of Mrs. Turner.

Jerry Boak, the mechanic that changed Hatch's oval tires on April 28th was also a key witness. He said he wondered why Hatch came to him to change the wide ovals when he knew Hatch worked at a station and could have changed them himself. He said Hatch paid cash for the work and asked the defendant, "How come your swapping them?" Hatch replied, "Gee, I got a good deal on these new ones and I thought I'd put them on."

Ted Wolff left little for Pawlinga to question when Joseph Nowak was under oath. He had him disclose his shady, criminal background and decided to let the jury know early on that his credibility was shaky, at best. The reaction by the defense was that he was a plant of the system that was prosecuting and an agent, hired or promised a plea for his pending felonies. The arguments went on for six days in closed sessions with the jury excused before Judge Walsh decided to allow his testimony and that he would not be considered a person who was placed in the jail as bait for a confession. When the jurors were questioned after the verdict, the opinion that allowed them to give Nowak credibility was the fact that he was being held in jail as a protected witness and his remuneration was five dollars a day. One juror commented that he wouldn't be held for 500 dollars a day.

The prosecution was stunned when the defense called the defendant to the stand and Ted started to shake his head in disbelief.. Hatch had taken the stand before in the rape case in Herkimer but his testimony was more in the form of a confession than an alibi. It was never determined whether it was the recommendation of counsel or the accused, but the move was risky since his prior criminal history became fair game and could be invoked by the prosecution.

Hatch spoke of his actions on the day of the murder, swearing that he was at a TV repair shop in Waterville after sleeping until noon.

It would be imprudent to review and describe the details of the trial any further. Having access to the summation as written by Ted Wolff would be the most accurate and unedited manner to describe how he was able to convince the jury that they had only one verdict to render- guilty. What follows is his formal summary that took 150 minutes to deliver.

"Ladies and gentlemen. On Thursday, April 26, 1973, James Weaver, a farmer on Potato Hill Road, Town of Steuben, saw a white object being dragged past his home by a green car. I suppose you have to put yourself in his position. The event was so strange and unusual that I doubt if he immediately realized the importance of what he observed. He felt that someone had been married, but the day and location would seem to say otherwise. He then thought that perhaps someone was dragging a deer or some other animal, but again, reason would tend to rule out that possibility. The thought that a car would be dragging a human being, tied up tight under the rear bumper would probably make the average person suspect their sanity. Whatever his thinking at the time, he continued working until late in the morning and it was not until he looked at the road, saw what he felt were drag marks, blood and intestines, followed the marks to Latteiman Road and talked to 5 or 6 people, that he decided the state police should be notified. This was about 3 to 3:30 in the afternoon. Trooper Jon Chaffee, now deceased, responded to the call and secured the evidence and went over the scene until dark. On Friday morning a group of troopers, led by Senior Investigator Thomas Gallagher went to the area, turned Weaver's home into a make shift command post and began their investigation.

After following the route that Weaver and Chaffee had traced and taking note of the drag marks and rope, seeing the recent fire in the turnaround, Gallagher called the District Attorney. I was at the time in charge of most homicides. Gallagher asked for me. He said, "You're not going to believe what I'm going to tell you." And he went on to tell me what had transpired. I had been trained to know that if you consider every death or possible death as a homicide until it is proven one way or the other, you can't make the mistake of minimizing any situation and therefore overlooking evidence which later turns out to be important. I drove to Steuben for almost two years and have been involved in the most intense and most bizarre investigation that Oneida County has ever seen.

I then decided that the only proper way to handle a major investigation and trial was to start out in the initial stages and work side by side with police officers and witnesses in order to have first hand knowledge, what, where and how. The defense would have you believe that Bernard Hatch was a suspect shortly after the investigation began, and I won't deny that, but will deny that he was the only suspect. What you have heard for three months and what is relevant, is the evidence that tends to prove that the defendant, Bernard Hatch, committed murder in that he intentionally caused the death of Mary Rose Turner.

Was the victim Mary Rose Turner? She wasn't seen alive after April 26, 1973. The following were found: rope with human blood, earrings, eyeglasses, rosary, lipstick case with mirror, cameo ring, comb, charred piece of blouse, part of a coat, motel key, a body identified by the family and matching blood, a right hand with a mother's ring, a left hand with a wedding ring. Tom Ash said there were not enough points in fingerprints to say it was Mrs. Turner, but it was his professional opinion that it was her. There is far too much evidence for anyone to doubt as to the identity or cause of death.

Where was Mary Turner during the early morning hours of April 26, 1973? She had physical problems, family problems, loneliness, an accident on the Thruway, had no car, didn't drink or frequent bars and didn't go to a friend's house. Mary Turner was on Court Street and around Bohling's Shell. She was seen by Ms. Jenny, Mrs. Fox, Walter Mikus, Robert Greely, Secor, Corelli, Cable and Edgar Frey. Did she have a connection with the station or defendant? She lived 10 blocks away on the same street, bought gas there, the station was opened all night, Simpson said she traded there. Mrs. Swider paid for her gas after her check bounced.

What was her connection with Hatch? She didn't have access to a car and didn't borrow one. She didn't walk to Steuben. It is obvious that the person who took her to Steuben and dragged her, knew the area well and was in Utica that morning. Hatch knew the area well, the dirt roads were difficult and driven by a person who knew them well. There were no homes in the area except for Weaver's and it appeared unlived in. Hatch left Utica between 8:15 to 8:30 a.m. The dragging was seen between 9:30a.m. and 10:30a.m. by a green car. Hatch's whereabouts were not proven or explained between 9a.m. and 1p.m. that day. Weaver, Stanco, Broadbent and Winters, described seeing a green car and described the driver by the photograph of Hatch.

Joseph Nowak says that on March 12 and March 22, 1974, in the County Jail, Hatch told him he dragged a girl behind his car and that he killed her, had committed a murder and was going to get away with it. The defense has told you that for three days during the trial, while Nowak was on the stand, about his background and marital problems.

The defense also spent at least 2 days attempting to show that Nowak was suicidal and could not have had that conversation since Hatch was in the afternoon class and not the evening. I won't deny that Joseph Nowak spent a good deal of his time in jail nor do I deny that he became upset about his wife to the point where he talked of suicide. Whatever his intention was, the history fits perfectly with his testimony as to the basis of the conversations. The testimony in the Winters case proved reliable and that Nowak did not receive any favors for his testimony. He was kept under guard as a material witness for seven months and didn't receive credit for "Good Time" during that period. There is also no evidence that Nowak refused or altered his testimony in any way the original information given to the state police. Please remember that it was Nowak's wife that first called the state police and notified them of the conversation and was not initiated by law enforcement.

What physical evidence tied Hatch to the crime? He was positively identified by the aforementioned. Hemp fibers on the hitch, the same fibers found at the gravesite. The search of the trunk of his car contained both the wool and acetate fibers found on the rope at the gravesite. The cloth found in the parking area of route 274 contained red paint, the same paint found in the jack of Hatch's car. The glove found on Potato Hill Road contained red paint, the same type glove given to the defendant by the mother of Linda Cady in 1970. The work pants recovered while the search warrant was executed contained spots of blood and red paint.

Evidence recovered from the trailer search. Found in the shed behind the trailer was a shovel with matched wool fiber that was identical to the fiber found at the cul-de-sac and the trunk of the defendant's car. There was also hair found attached to the rope that matched Mary Rose Turner's hair. There was also a pair of dark shoes with traces of blood on the left shoe and a spot of blood on the right shoe. Although his brother-in-law said they were his shoes and not the defendant's, they both wear size 10. There were also nine hairs found on the sole of the right shoe adhering to the blood spot. When you consider how the hairs adhered, the blood was not dry but wet and sticky at the time. The nine hairs were identified as Mary Rose Turner's, testified by Ms. Howarth as having the same razor cut as given to the deceased. A knife sheath was found in the dresser drawer of the defendant's bedroom during the search. It contained two hairs which matched the known hair of the deceased. You may recall Dr. Thomas' testimony when he said the legs and hand were severed with a sharp instrument and that any of the knives recovered could have done it, including the one in the sheath where hairs were found.

What were the activities of the defendant before and after the incident? On April 28, 1973, a Saturday, Hatch changed two of his tires. He kept the newspaper clippings of the grave discovery in his dresser drawer. He denied knowing anything about the homicide when he discussed it with Mr. Wilson at work, despite the fact he had driven past the troop cars and must have heard or seen the S.P. helicopter making passes all day Saturday and Sunday. Four days after the murder he spoke to Christine Chappel that he was laying low for a few days and afraid the police would pick him up.

Hatch's alibi. Florence Hatch, mother of the defendant, testified that John Pulcini got up about 9:30a.m. and left with Victoria, Hatch's sister, to take a TV to Waterville and get her car. She stated that the defendant got up after 11a.m. on Thursday the 24th. This was about the same time Joyce Burdick said she saw him. About the same time, John and Victoria said they came back to the trailer and they all left for Dodge City between 11:30a.m. and noon. On May 15, Investigator Peo interviewed the defendants mother and she told him that her son slept until 12:30p.m or 1:00 p.m. and then everyone left for Dodge City. They gave Tom Carl the following time line:

Original times		Told T. Carl	
John	Victoria	John	Victoria
Got up 9 a.m.	9:15-9:30	10:30	10:30
Left 9:30	9:30	11:00	11:15
Home 11:30	11:15-11:30	2 p.m.	1 p.m.
Left 11:45	11:45-11:55	2:30	1:15
Left 11:50	11:40-12:00	3:00	1:30

Remember, Mrs. Hatch, John and Victoria at all times refused to sign any statements or submit to a polygraph. The most important point to consider is why is there such a discrepancy in time? Why do all the three members of the Hatch family move the clock back 1 ½ to 2 hours and why do their good friends, the Snyder's, remember seeing the defendant at 11:45, going towards Utica when 9 days after the murder they couldn't recall them seeing him at all? The answer is obvious and should play an important part in your deliberations. The answer is Earl Winters and Stephen Earl. On May 20 and 21, 1974, there were hearings held in this court. These were the suppression hearings Mr. Pawlinga referred to often and used testimony from. At those hearings, it was the first time the defendant found out that Mr. Winters and Mr. Earl had seen his car on Latteiman Road, not far from the gravesite, and it was April 24, 1973 at 11:50 a.m. They also learned for the first time that both men saw car photos and picked out the defendant's car, but what is more important is that Mr. Earl had picked out Hatch's car from a group of photos. This is why the times had to change to cover the 11:15 time. What better way to have the defendant 10 miles away going in the opposite direction. Can you accept the testimony of witnesses who have made statements in the past so completely different and who, although they claim the complete innocence of the defendant? One other little problem that was forgotten was Anne Alsheimer. She testified that she didn't open until noon and recalled that the Pulcini's didn't come until later in the afternoon and signed a statement to that affect on May 16, 1973. The family, of course, made one last effort to explain this, but again, Mrs. Alsheimer came back and said she recalled no such telephone call and even if there had been one, she wouldn't have opened except for family or close personal friends and the Hatch's and Pulcini's didn't fit either category. Use your own judgment and give these alibis and testimony, the amount of consideration it deserves.

As to the rest of the defense, I don't feel that the attempt of Anthony Mastracco to discredit the state police, or for the defense to infer that Robert Cable killed Mary Turner because she used to fight with his girlfriend are worthy of comment. Neither is the attempt by Howard Bohling to infer that a woman was struggling with two males in a car near Utica Club Brewery. These are cheap shots that are used to smoke up the real issues.

Can you believe the testimony of the defense witnesses when you add to it the criminal record of the defendant in Herkimer County when he tied up two people and used a weapon? They, the defense attorney in that case said that all they had was two witnesses who identified Hatch's car, the weapon being found in his car that matched the shell casing at the scene, and that was all. What's enough? I leave it to you whether the defendant is lying or extremely naïve.

In closing, I leave it to you to make one conclusion. If Bernard Hatch didn't kill Mary Turner then someone who looks just like him, with a car just like his and with the same extraordinary knowledge of the area, is the guilty party. This would stretch even my imagination to the breaking point, since to believe this you would have to eliminate all of the physical evidence from your mind.

As I told you when we started, this was basically a circumstantial evidence case. I wonder if you have stopped to consider that had Weaver called the state police at 9:30 or so when he first saw the car dragging something, this would not have been a case of circumstantial evidence. A member of the state police would have responded and definitely seen the car and the body before the burial could have been completed. I show this only to show the thin line between a direct evidence case and a so called circumstantial case.

Certain members of the state police, Tom Carl in particular and myself have worked on this case for about two years now, and remember this: that during this entire two years you do not stop working on the case because you go home at night, take a day off or go on vacation. You live with it day and night and it haunts you because I know, as a prosecutor, that ultimately the entire investigation comes down to this-the trial and the jury deliberation. Can you imagine what it's like to live with that, knowing that you have the responsibility of setting up the case and trying it and if you make an error in judgment, this defendant who committed this horrible crime may go free? Now that part is over. I have tried the case as well as I could. I gave you everything that is pertinent from the total investigation. I don't know how many mistakes I've made, only your verdict will determine that. I will tell you this-if you feel from the evidence the defendant is innocent, then somehow I have made a very serious error. I have failed to show you what I personally feel, that this defendant is guilty.

I asked you in opening not to pick the evidence apart, leave that to Mr. Pawlinga. Consider all the evidence as one total picture and then decide where that leaves you and what the picture shows.

You can't do anything for Mary Rose Turner but you can do something for me and for you and for all the people in the county and the state. If you carefully consider all the evidence, that evidence warrants a conviction and justice demands it."

Judge John J. Walsh didn't use a standard charge for the jury, he'd write everyone individually after he made an appraisal of what the jurors would understand. He was a brilliant but common person and never spoke in "Legaleze." He started with how important their duty is since they are determining the fate and the life of a person accused of murder. He inserted the words "sound judgment and in good conscience." He reduced their decision to simplicity, either guilty or innocent. Reminding them that punishment is not their concern, it belongs to the judge's area of responsibility. Reminding them of the presumption of innocence and the burden on the prosecution and how inferences are in favor of the defendant. Weighing the evidence, reasonable doubt was then touched upon. He described reasonable doubt as, "An honest doubt based upon the state of the evidence adduced against a person, or upon the lack, failure or insufficiency of the evidence."

It was apparent that the charge was favoring the defendant, which it should. He used the words "Unpleasant and distasteful" as he continued and metaphorically, "Placed the ball in the prosecutors court." The search for the truth was emphasized and said that they were the sole judges of the facts, with no scientific tests to guide them. Form your own impressions as to their credibility but consider whether the witness had a motive which may have influenced their testimony. Since the defendant opted to take the stand, he said he should be treated as they would any other witness and balance the weight and credibility of their testimony. He was clear on speaking of police officers testimony and admonished them that their credence is held to the same standard as all witnesses, without distinction, there isn't a double standard.

He defined an expert witness, qualifications, education and said they were to be treated as any other witness, considering the opinions, weigh the opinions, either accept or reject and not be bound by the concluding opinion.

Bouncing the ball into the defense's court he may have alluded to Nowak's testimony when he said, "Now, if a witness be shown to have a bad reputation generally, for truth and veracity, it does not necessarily follow that he is untruthful in this instance. It is a collateral matter which the jury may consider in determining the weight to be given to his testimony." His conclusion was, "It is important to remember that the court has no opinion as to the guilt or innocence of a defendant. This is your sole responsibility."

The jury was sequestered but not for long. They found for the prosecution, guilty of murder, 2nd degree. Ted did not feel a "Serious error."

The sentencing minutes were curt. Judge Walsh felt that a condemnation of the juries decision was overkill, the sentence would tell it all. The courtroom was silenced as Judge Walsh spoke. "In imposing sentence in this case, the court wishes to make only a brief statement. In accordance with our usual practice, the court does not express any personal opinion as to the guilt or innocence of a defendant, as this is the sole and exclusive function of a jury. When the jury had made a determination of guilt, it becomes the duty of the court to impose a sentence.

In the case of murder, the statute itself mandates the maximum sentence of life imprisonment. It also provides that the court must set a minimum period of imprisonment of from fifteen to twenty-five years. This permits the court to take into consideration any significant or extenuating circumstances in a particular case.

Here, if the defendant is actually innocent as he maintains, and this will be subjected to appellate review of the entire case, then the sentence is unfair both to the defendant and society, generally. On the other hand, if the defendant actually committed the crime, as the jury had found, this court is at a loss to find, in view of the gruesome nature of the homicide, any extenuating circumstances which would warrant any lesser sentence than that permitted by law."

Chapter 11

The Unsuccesful Appeal

Bernard Hatch's mother was a devoted lady and had, what some described, as an abnormal affinity for her son, regardless of his predilection to murdering innocent people. Some say the bond was created by being nursed until he was five years old, others think it was caused by his abusive father. Florence Hatch was the deeded owner of a lot and a home in Forestport, N.Y. in the foothills of the Adirondack Mountains, She called it "Her camp." Her granddaughter said it was worth $20,000. His mother bought it in 1961 and stayed there often in the summer and early fall months.

Soon after Hatch's conviction Florence inquired about an appeal, feeling it was an injustice. Mr. Pawlinga told her that there was a lot of work and research and it would cost $20,000., with no guarantee it would succeed. Five years, and eight months later, she deeded the camp to his lawyer for $1.00 and other good and valuable considerations. Pawlinga ,got the appeal money or like kind and quality. He affected the appeal in February, 1983.

Mr .Pawlinga raised and would argue the following:

1) The Trial Court abused its discretion
2) The cross-examination of the defendant was improper
3) The defendant was denied the right to a fair trial
4) The prosecution did not provide copies of a statement of a witness.
5) The evidence was insufficient to support the conviction of murder

The proper venue for this appeal was the Appellate Court of the Supreme Court in New York State. Since the site of the trial was

Oneida County, the Fourth Judicial Department had jurisdiction and would be argued in Rochester. The Appellate Court is considered the intermediate level of appeals, the highest court being, The Court of Appeals. This would be the second motion the court would hear on The People of the State of New York v. Hatch. The first argument, which was denied by the five judges, occurred on October, 18, 1974, before a jury was paneled.

The question for the 1974 appeal was a request for a change of venue and the defense attorney maintained that there was reasonable cause to believe that a fair and impartial trial cannot be held in Oneida County. The central issue was that the defendant would suffer from the adverse publicity the crime had caused and his prior conviction would make it impossible to seat an impartial jury. The rejection was unanimous.

The Appellate Department has the authority to review, not only the law, but also the facts. The Court of Appeals may only rule on the law. Judge Walsh didn't worry about the merits of the 1983 appeal and was relatively sure he wouldn't be reversed by his decisions and the proof he allowed to be entered. After the briefs were filed and placed on the calendar, they both, the defense and the prosecutor were allowed fifteen minutes each to summarize their case. It is interesting to note that the U.S. Supreme Court restricts the oral arguments to thirty minutes for each party

Donald Gerace, Assistant District Attorney, was delegated by the D.A. to prepare the brief and argue the case, why it shouldn't be reversed. Mr. Gerace was a methodical and careful lawyer with a penchant for detail and research and shared Judge Walsh's optimism for success. He would be ably assisted in his preparation by Ted Wolff. Mr. Pawlinga was not to be underestimated, he'd be well prepared also, respected and attentive to detail.

Mr. Gerace skillfully devoted endless hours crafting his brief, outlining and editing his challenges, knowing the gravity of the adverse result if freed or a demand for a new trial. He developed a logical time-line of events: investigation, cross-examination, refusal of the change of venue, Joseph Nowak's testimony, Weaver's statement and lastly a provocative argument as to the merits of Judge Walsh's decisions and why the lower court should be affirmed.

ADA Gerace included in the Appendix of his brief, thought to be a stroke of legal genius, under sub (E) an affidavit by Edward A. Wolff Jr. dated February 17, 1983, masked as the reasonable basis for cross-examination. It reviewed inclusions that were not within the purview of the appeal and may have been overlooked or disregarded as pertinent by Mr. Pawlinga. The contents of the sworn statement were startling and had to sway the judges as to the heinousness of the crime. He was able to sneak in the five point questions asked of Hatch when he took the stand. They were:

1) The alleged shooting of a neighbor's cow by Hatch
2) His wife's visit at the Oneida County Jail, arriving in good spirits and leaving in an extremely upset condition and committing suicide later that same evening.
3) That Hatch shot a cat with a .45, in Washington Mills, N.Y.
4) That Hatch admitted to his wife that he had killed someone during his tour of duty in the Marine Corps.
5) That Hatch had threatened to kill his wife on one or more occasions.

The cow incident was supported by a conversation between Wolff and Myron Senchyna, who witnessed it. The visit to the jail, by his wife, was corroborated by a conversation between Wolff the jail personnel, the investigators and Coroner when responding to the suicide. Shooting the cat and the murder while in the Marine Corps were attributed to an interview with Mrs. Hatch and Major Charland , who was with the BCI at the time, investigating a kidnapping, rape and sodomy, in 1963. Written notes and sworn statements bolstered Wolff's questions.

An additional legal gift he possessed was to slip in to the Appendix, although not fundamental to the rebuttal of the appeal, Exhibit A, titled "Autopsy Report" a five page gruesome detail of the results of the slaughter of Mary Rose Turner. The final diagnosis was glaring as the words reported:

1) Dismembered body
2) Marked mutation of body, apparently secondary to dragging.
3) Loss of vital organs

4) Lower extremities, received separately
5) Upper extremities received separately
6) Cause of death, asphyxia, secondary to strangulation
7) The body has been largely eviscerated
8) There is a rope mark about the neck
9) Missing are: spleen, small intestine, stomach
10) It is not possible to see both the lungs and the heart

The transcribed minutes of Hatch's testimony (page 5693) were crucial to the success of the defense of the appeal. The defendant was asked by Wolff, as the trial wound down, whether or not the police were suspicious of him because the people he associated with had a tendency to disappear. Hatch never responded to the inquiry.

Nowak's testimony was the linchpin for the prosecution's case. Although a convicted felon, the conversation with Hatch in the jail was given credibility by the jury. Wolff asked the witness whether he had a conversation with Hatch in the rec room of the jail, Pawlinga objected and a session behind closed doors continued for three days. There were 650 pages of testimony and arguments produced and the ultimate ruling by Judge Walsh was that Nowak's statements could be heard and the jury given the responsibility as to the veracity.

Attorney Gerace called the victory, the success of the prosecutor and the presiding judge, the most gratifying moment of his legal career. He began his vocation after graduating from Siena College and then Albany Law School by working in Jefferson County in Northern New York as an Assistant D.A. He chose to begin a private practice in 1988 in Utica. He was modest about winning the appeal and mentioned a parallel between a serial killer, Lemuel Smith and Bernard Hatch. It was during an internship while in Albany Law School when he recalled vividly an exposure to Smith who was being arraigned for the murder of a female correction officer in a Downstate prison. He said Smith had the same aura about him as did Hatch, eerie and ghostly. It would be a safe assumption that the denial of the appeal has been instrumental in precluding release on parole.

Chapter 12

MISSING PERSONS

The Utica Police Department has a missing persons department, the Juvenile Aid Division. The "subject" classified the discovery of Linda and Lisa Cady as, "Unidentified body found at Town of Steuben." Gene Williams was the police officer who submitted the following to Chief Rotundo.

"Ordered by Rotundo (Cannistra and Bush) to assist the New York State Police relative to finding a body on Potato Hill, Town of Steuben.

Dorothea Aiken states that she had not heard from her granddaughter since she had reported them missing. She gave us the name of Dr. Sapia as her dentist and that she had not been treated by him since she was a young girl. We then interviewed Dr. Sapia at his office and he gave us a full chart on Cady-Aiken. Information turned over to T. Carl, NYSP. Subject not located. This complaint is being referred to the Open Missing file.

Mrs. Aiken, 610 Albany St. reported to UPD that her daughter (22) and her 3 year old daughter Lisa, were missing from home since 6/20/70. At the time of the report she said that her daughter had left a note stating that she was moving to Syracuse to find a job. Teletype 784 was sent out on the missing subjects and all cars were alerted. The writer spoke to friends of the missing subject and their family and that no one had any knowledge other than the fact that Bernard Hatch, who worked at the Bohling Shell was her boyfriend. The writer spoke to Mr. Hatch who stated that he hadn't seen the subject for sometime and heard that she had left the area. Interview of Dorothea Aiken: Hatch and Linda starting dating in the summer of 1969. They went steady until 1 week before June 20, 1970. Dorothea didn't like Hatch, he showed more attention to Lisa Ann than to Linda. She would spend

89

weekends at Hatch's mother's in Deansboro or at camp in Forestport or at the Pulcini trailer. Hatch helped Ms. Aiken paint the parlor. Saw Hatch on Monday June 22, 1970, Hatch said he had a wild weekend, had scratches on his left cheek and jaw. Linda always wore a wig. Didn't take it to Syracuse with her." When the corpses were found on December 8, there wasn't an identification as to who they were. When the Utica Police Department received notification, two investigators were detailed to interview the family of Lorraine Zinicola, one of the two families that were logged as missing. The interview will be documented under the Zinicola discussion. On December 11, 1973, the missing persons file on the Cady's was cancelled after identification was made by the pathologist, the archeologist and the coroner.

The special file contained follow up data on the relationship of Hatch and Linda. "The writer spoke to a friend of the missing subject and her family and it was learned that no one had any knowledge other than the fact that Bernard Hatch, who worked at the Bohling Shell Station on Court and State St., was her boyfriend. The writer spoke to Mr. Hatch who stated that he hadn't seen the subject for sometime and heard that she left the area. A friend of Linda's, Shirley Bills, stated that on June 18, 1970, a Friday, Hatch had picked up Linda in the early afternoon. On the same day at 2:30 p.m. Linda drew $345.00 out of a savings account at the Oneida National Bank on Mohawk Street in Utica. Bills further stated that, 'He'll (Hatch) kill her if she left him and didn't do what he wanted her to do.'"

Further proof of the relationship was supported by Georgena Laymon who said that Linda had spoken to her about the possibility of her being pregnant and that Hatch didn't want the baby. On June 22, 1970, Bills and Linda's mother go to Syracuse, speak to a friend of Linda's, Wanda (nee Dunn) Stepello searching for Linda. On the same date, a fellow worker of Hatch named Chapple, observes Hatch at 7:00 a.m. and he had scratches on his face. Charles Aiken corroborated Chapple's statement. The friendship between Linda and Wanda was close enough for Linda to confide in her on Easter, 1970. Linda said that she needed a psychiatrist as "Hoss" as she called him, ditched her. She spoke of the punishment he inflicted and had beaten her up. On January 11, 1970, Linda went to Syracuse and shared, for most of the night, how much she loved Hoss, but was jealous of his ex wife, Andrea and that she resented him spending so much time with Cassandra. She said that she would eventually marry Hatch.

Charles Aiken was questioned by the N.Y.S.P. on May 2, 1973. He knew of the relationship between Cady and Hatch and recalled it was late '69, early '70's. He said the relationship cooled off in June '70 because he wouldn't marry her. He knew that they would spend week ends together at the Pulcini trailer in Steuben.

An un-mailed letter recovered in Cady's home on Albany Street contained the following, addressed to Gloria Lopez, Chicago: " Isn't it funny we were practically married and had our children on the same day. Lucky for you, your marriage turned out better than mine. I'm going with this guy named Bernie Hatch, we call him Hoss. He's not a sex-fiend like my ex-husband. I have a healthy, loving daughter and she loves Hoss like he's her own father and he treats her like she's his own. He treats me good too. I'm pretty sure I love him but I'm a little doubtful about getting involved because of the mess I made of my first marriage. I feel safe and happy when I'm with him and I never felt that way with_____-. Kiss the kids for me. Enough of my life. Love, Linda."

The state police continued in their hunt for the Zinicola family. On May 4, 1974, Investigators Friedman and Doyle interviewed Mrs. Victoria Penar, the mother of Lorraine, the grandmother of her three boys. They had picked her up at her home and she accompanied them to Troop D Headquarters. She was 64 at the time and lived at 1002 Sunset Avenue, Utica. Children's clothing were found in the Potato Hill area by the search detail. Asking her to identify them as belonging to her grandchildren failed as she said she didn't recognize the clothing. She did go through the litany of when she last saw the family, 8:30 a.m. July 9, 1971. She said her daughter was going on a trip and that the day before she had withdrawn $4,000.00 from a joint savings account from Cornhill Savings and Loan. She had spoken to Lorraine's friends since that date and no one had heard from her.

On the same date, May 4, Investigator Arcuri made a trip to the DMV to check the records of automobiles owned by Hatch and Zinicola. The following is the production of ownership:

Hatch:	'62 Oldsmobile, 2 door, black, VIN 626L06613
	'64 Oldsmobile, 2 door, black, VIN 874L03617
Lorraine:	'68 Oldsmobile, convertible, red, 344678H
	'61 Oldsmobile, 4 door, green, 612L06412

Tracing the title and records revealed that on **JUNE 5, 1971, Lorraine sold the 1968 Oldsmobile to Bernard Hatch and on the same date a transaction occurred between Hatch and Zinicola selling her one of his registered cars. She was seen leaving her home on 7/9/71 with the car she had purchased from Hatch.** Hatch had an affection for Oldsmobiles, better described as an obsession. The vehicles observed in May 1974 were: Black sedan, Olds, white sedan, Olds, Blue sedan, Olds, another blue Olds sedan.

Lorraine Vennaro, age 28 at the time, living at 5 Kernan Avenue, Whitesboro, was interviewed by Arcuri. She considered Zinicola as her best friend, bowling together and socializing. She worked at the Department of Licensing. She said that there was a deep affection between the two and that Hatch was "Attached" to the three boys. She added that Zinicola and Hatch would use each others cars on occasion. In 1991, the author called Ms. Vennaro and set up a time and place to be interviewed. The night before we were to meet, she called and said she wouldn't talk to me and that she was afraid of Hatch.

The grandmother said that Lorraine placed two suitcases in her '61 Olds, was wearing a pear shaped chain with gold trim around her neck with a watch dangling from it. She said her daughter wore a 10 or 12 clothes size and she packed her belongings in a beige suitcase with the initials L.A.P. a Sampsonite. She described the second suitcase as blue.

The car was never recovered.

AFTERWORD

Criminal History

Avoidance and protection of rape victims identity is sacred. It is a humane and delicate law that should be embraced by the media and anyone reporting any details such as names, and we will maintain the anonymity of the victims in our first two scenarios of Hatch's criminal career.

On October 25, 1963, while home on leave from the Marine Corps and staying in Utica, New York, he decided to "cruise around" and ended up in Frankfort Gorge, 12 miles from where he was staying. The Gorge Road, as it is referred to, is lightly traveled and unlit. Hatch came upon a lane off of the paved highway and saw a car parked about 100 feet from the road.. In the car there was a young couple, a 16 year old female and her eighteen year old boyfriend who was home on leave from the Army. Hatch forced them out of the car at gunpoint. .He tied both parties to trees, a few yards apart ,and took the male's wallet from his pocket and discarded it when he found it empty. He then performed a loathsome sexual act on the teenage girl, fired a warning shot over the head of her boyfriend, untied the girl and left with her, sobbing, in his car. The victims placed the time at between 8:30 and 9:15 p.m. Hatch then drove to Sauquoit N,Y. about 10 miles southeast of the Gorge, raped the girl and drove her to her home in Frankfort, arriving at 12:30 a.m.

The make, color and plate number of the car was called into the Herkimer Barracks of the State Police and in the early morning hours of October 26, 1963. Investigator Charland of the State Police BCI, made the arrest, had Hatch arraigned. in Herkimer County and held on $15,000 bail. It is unimaginable, but true, that the Observer Dispatch, the Utica paper, printed the victim's name and age (16) which in today's arena, she would have been protected from disclosure because of her age and being a rape victim.

On July 16, 1964, Hatch was tried for a host of felonies: kidnapping, robbery 1st, abduction, possession of a firearm, possession of a loaded firearm and rape 1. The District Attorney, Albert Schneider, had an easy time convicting the jury of his guilt as he paraded the victim, Troopers Boall, Gerbracht, Carl and investigators Restante, Dennis, Brefka and Charland before the judge and jury and after 5 hours of deliberation they found him guilty on all counts with the exception of robbery and abduction. The sentence was 25 to life, all counts to run concurrent and revoked bail.

Despite his attorney's admonition not to take the stand before sentencing, Hatch was sworn in and stated, " My name is Bernard Philip Hatch (Hoss) AKA Bob Cole. I was born in Goshen, New York. I am stationed at Camp Lejeune Marine Corps Base. I am 24 years old, born 3/5/40 and I have practiced the trade of motor mechanic. I am Protestant and married. My mother is living and I have gone to the 9th grade. I am temperate in my habits and I have no previous convictions. I know of no legal cause to show why judgment of the court should not be pronounced against me."

On January 3, 1967, after serving 3 plus years in Attica Correctional Facility, his attorney, George Krohn, applied to the U.S. Supreme Court for a writ of certiorari.

Translated, it means that he requested an appellate review to determine whether there were any irregularities. He was classified as a "Deserter'" by the Marine Corps until he was convicted and then a mandatory Dishonorable Discharged was issued by the Department of Navy.

Represented by an assigned counsel, his conviction and sentence was argued before the Appellate Division, 4th Department and on February 17, 1966, the kidnapping charge was dismissed and the other charges affirmed. The alternative sentences were: abduction, 1 to 10 years, gun charges, 3 and one half to 7 years, to run concurrent. The basis for the reversal was the legality of the search and seizure, identification of the defendant, absence of a lineup and prejudicial remarks by the District Attorney during the summation. The decision also criticized the judge's charge to the jury. Hatch was released from Attica under Parole Supervision. His Parole Officer would be Robert Wozna. His parole expiration date was October 20, 1973. After three years in

Attica he was relatively free to roam the streets and seek his next prey. The Department of Correctional Services (DOCS) has his Intelligence Quotient listed as 107. This made him a little above the average. His next arrest was in January, 1972. In concert with the protection we would afford to the identity of rape victims, the name of the person raped will be shielded. We'll give her another name, "Debbie."

It was close to midnight and Hatch had just left work at the gas station. Blustery and frigid, the thermometer read 10 degrees above zero. Debbie had an argument with her live- in boyfriend and left in an impulsive rage bringing her three year old daughter with her. They were both scantily dressed, hardly enough clothing to protect her and her daughter from the biting cold. Living a block from the Arterial, as it was called, she was destined to achieve a safe haven in Frankfort with a friend who would house her. Without transportation she opted to hitchhike, which she had done before. Standing on the shoulder of the highway she extended her clasped hand with the thumb open and hugging her daughter with her free arm.

A helpful motorist, she thought, stopped and beckoned her into the car. It was Hatch," cruising," again and looking for someone to victimize. She enjoyed the warmth and began small talk with the driver. She became querulous when she said she was going to Frankfort and he continued north on the Arterial, route 12 , instead of going east on route 5. About 6 miles north of where she gained; what she thought was safety, Hatch pulled off on a desolate road and parked the car, leaving the motor running. Debbie grabbed her daughter, and fled the car but was stopped by Hatch and forced back into the rear seat

Hatch displayed a knife, held it close to the baby's throat and told Debbie to undress.

According to her testimony, he raped her twice as her daughter sobbed in the front seat. He then drove Debbie and her baby to her intended destiny in Frankfort. Debbie elected not to report it immediately. It was three weeks later after a gynecological exam, that she was prompted by the doctor to report her history to the police as she related it to him. When she completed a report to the Utica Police Officer, the investigator asked the same question, "Why did you wait so long to report it?"

Through identification of the car, the plate number and the description of the assailant, a warrant was issued for Bernard Paul Hatch and in March, 1972 he was tried for rape in the first degree. Ted Wolff, the Senior Prosecutor for the D.A's Office was given the dubious assignment, with misgivings about the success. He knew that the conviction hinged on the uncorroborated testimony of the victim and her demeanor. In 1972 the prior sexual history of the complainant was admissible. Today, 2008, it isn't. She was a thirty two year old mother with four children born out of wedlock, and under intense cross examination by the defense attorney, Steve Pawlinga, she couldn't recall the names of the fathers of her children. She was a prosecutor's worse nightmare and a defense attorney's dream. Wolff schooled Debbie and reviewed the questions he'd ask and the appropriate answers she'd deliver. He also told her how to dress: long skirt or dark slacks, buttoned blouse limited makeup. Refusing his urging and recommendations, she took the stand with: too much makeup, mini skirt, high heels, purple nails and an ankle bracelet. Her appearance was destructive, her testimony a disaster. She said she entered his car willingly after soliciting the ride, she didn't resist penetration and recited waiting three weeks before she reported it to the police. Her testimony included the statement, "I'd do anything he wanted me to do because I was scared. I struggled, fought and screamed pretty loud when he tried to kiss me." She described and pointed to Hatch as he sat staring at her. During the direct by Wolff and the cross by Pawlinga she said, "He had a long bushy beard, sideburns, big and strong, gentle voice," and as she\pointed to her attacker she said that he was sitting in the court room clean shaven. The prosecutor realized that it would take a miracle for him to obtain a conviction .

The crowning blow was when Pawlinga's summation included the following words to the already dubious jurors as he raised his eyes toward the ceiling, outstretched his arms and increased the volume

in his voice, almost shouting, "Ladies and gentlemen of the jury, can you convict a man of rape, send him to prison for his natural life on the uncorroborated testimony of that woman?" pointing to the complainant. He continued, " C'mon now, Ladies and Gentlemen, do you really believe she was raped? Come now." As he sauntered to his chair, he gave the prosecutor a wink, knowing he had a victory, and he was right.

After two and a half hours of deliberation they found Hatch innocent. It was small consolation for the victim and the prosecutor that Hatch wasn't set free but remanded to the Oneida County Jail pending a parole violation hearing. Wolff wondered why Hatch had the right to rape Debbie in the presence of her child and be freed merely because the unwed mother had no fashion sense. He had a convoluted hunch that this would not be the last time he would meet Bernard Hatch and Steve Pawlinga in the courtroom. His conjecture was accurate but not consoling. Ted Wolff was not a good loser. He mused the adage, "Winning isn't everything

Linda Cady was born on November 27, 1947 to Dorothea and Charles Aiken. Her only child, Lisa Ann, was born on August 22, 1966. On December 8, 1973, both of their bodies were discovered in shallow graves in a wooded area off Latteiman Road in Steuben, New York. The last time they were seen alive was Saturday, June 20, 1970.

Linda's father Charles died in 1951 at the age of 31. Linda had two younger brothers, Richard and Dale. Seven months before the hideous discovery, May 2, 1973, as the Troopers were continuing their search for evidence involving the Turner murder, they came upon some clothing on the north side of Latteiman Road under a spruce tree. It was about a football field away from where Mary Rose was unearthed and a half mile from Potato Hill Road. It was apparent that her clothes were discarded and described as female adult and child's clothes. The I.D. team performed their perfunctory task: photograph, tag, bag and secure the evidence. Thus began the chain of custody.

Since Lisa and Linda Cady were on the missing persons log for years, the B.C.I were dispatched to take the recovered clothing to Linda's family for identification, 610 Albany Street, Utica. The garments were: a pair of ladies slacks called "Knee Knockers", also culottes, (cut off and cuffed at the knee), 2 night gowns (pink and yellow, 2 piece green bathing suit, dark blue sweater, a blue child's nylon jacket and two night gowns, rotted, frayed and indistinguishable. The Knee Knockers, white with orange-white lines, were immediately identified as belonging to Linda. Positive ID of the bathing suit was made by her brother as he was with her when she bought it and he helped her pick it out.

Mrs. Aiken left the living room sobbing, knowing that something dramatic and eerie had happened to her only daughter and her child. The process was not consoling but a form of preparation for what hey felt was inevitable, Linda and Lisa were probably dead.

A note was discovered by her mother, undated soon after Linda had left and never delivered saying, "Mom; I decided I needed a change. I've been thinking about it quite a while and heard about a couple of jobs in Syracuse and decided to take one. I have enough money to take care of myself. It is best for all of us, so there won't be anymore fights or arguments. Don't worry about me, I'll be better my own and I can handle it. I will write to you when I'm settled,. I love you. Linda. p.s. I appreciate all you have done for me."

Linda's mother and a friend, Shirley Bills drove to Syracuse to ask another of Linda's friends, Wanda Stepello, whether they saw or heard from Linda. They hadn't. Dorothea went to the Syracuse Police Station to report a missing persons and they refused ,saying she wasn't within their jurisdiction.

Linda and Bernard Hatch were not having a tryst, it was an open and passionate romance. According to Dorothea, Linda was dating Hatch from the summer of 1969 until she left, or was reported missing, on June 20, 1970. Linda's friend Shirley Bills, told the NYSP Investigator that Hatch had picked up Linda and Lisa Ann in the early afternoon of Thursday, June 18, 1970. On Friday, June 19, 1970, as the records reflect, Linda withdrew $345.00 from her savings account at the Oneida National Bank on Mohawk Street in Utica. She was there at 2:30 p.m. Combined with her note that she was going to Syracuse to live, it may have been enough for a months rent in an apartment.

The description of Linda given to the Utica P.D. by her mother read, "Missing since 6/20/70, reported 7/2/70, 2 p.m., Linda Cady, 610 Albany St. Utica, N.Y. 5'-5 1/2"- 130lbs., hazel eyes, brown hair, complexion; fair, build -thin, glasses, teeth-good, nose-n arrow. Could be in Syracuse with three year old daughter." After being exhumed, this description was of little value. The night before she was discovered missing by the family, she called one of her girlfriends and told her she was pregnant. Linda's brother Rick told the Utica P.D. that on June 20, 1970, he received a telephone call from Linda and said, "Make sure Mom gets my note." He described her emotional state as, "Nervous, really ill at ease." He also added that she didn't bring very many clothes with her and didn't think he'd be leaving for an extended period, maybe just an overnight. Pawing trough her personal belongings they found that her divorce decree was missing.

Myron Szychena was interviewed after the bodies were uncovered and identified. He was a neighbor of Hatch's sister Victoria and her husband John Pulcini and he stated that he was at the Pulcini's trailer on June 20th and that Linda and Lisa were there in the afternoon and about 4 p.m. Hatch left and said he was going to visit his daughter and ex-wife. Linda didn't drive and Myron said he had seen Linda and Lisa earlier but not at 4 o'clock when Hatch departed the trailer. John and Victoria had left the trailer to do some shopping.

Sunday, June 21, Hatch was scheduled to work the late shift at Bohling's Shell, A fellow worker, Joseph Chapple answered he phone about 4 p.m. It was Hatch and Chapple thought he sounded drunk. Hatch said he was having personal problems, he was in Watertown and would miss his shift. He asked if Harry Wilson would work his shift for him. The S.P. file relates an interview with another fellow employee, Charles Aiken, not related to Linda. He recalled seeing Hatch on June 22, a Monday ,and recalls asking Hatch about the scratches on his jaw and left cheek. Hatch's explanation was, "Charlie, I had a wild weekend"."

Dorothea was convinced Hatch killed her daughter and granddaughter. She knew the romance had it's rocky moments and she hoped that someday Hatch would, "Get the chair."

Ted Wolff was confident he had gathered sufficient evidence that Hatch murdered and dismembered Linda and Lisa, even if it was circumstantial evidence. That's why the arrest warrant was prepared to be served if Hatch was exonerated in the Turner murder.

What was perplexing to Sergeant Roman and Wolff was the motive to kill the Cady's. Ted felt that she had told Hatch she was pregnant and in a demented passion decided he didn't want to be a father again and his resolution was to eliminate her and her baby.

The autopsy couldn't determine whether Linda was pregnant or not. In today's world, 2008, many states have held that if a pregnant mother is killed, the murderer would be charged with a double homicide.

Sergeant Roman meditated about the sequence, did the mother see her daughter killed or did the daughter watch her mother lain?

Coincidentally, Trooper Jon Chaffee was killed in an auto accident the week before the bodies of the Cady's were found.

The morning newspaper, the Daily Press on January 13 headlined "Student slain on South Park Drive," The first person to be interviewed by the Utica Police Department was Bernard Paul Hatch. The gruesome murder occurred on Wednesday, January 12, 1972.The neighborhood and the City of Utica were terrorized. As of this date the case remains unsolved and open. Most State Police and Utica Police still maintain it was the M.O. (Modus operandi-method of operation) of Hatch. It had his signature on the murder.

Hatch had a frail alibi that day, he was working at Bohling's Shell Station and the time cards verified his presence. The headlines said, "Police hunt 20 year old in gold car." Ted Wolff thought ,and echoed by Sergeant Roman, that the time cards didn't reflect Hatch taking cars that he had worked on for what was called a "Test drive." Test driving after repairs were made, was common practice at Bohling's Shell Station, where he worked.

Joanne Pecheone had taken a bus home from school, De Sales High School in Utica, three miles from her home. After leaving the bus she took what was called a "short cut" to her home on Lin Road. It was a path that saved walkers time and a direct route to Lin Road and Nob Road. It was a wooded incline and identified by the neighbors as a popular parking area for couples and also a snowmobile path. Her body was found by a 12 year old snowmobiler about 4:00 p.m, David Inserra ,who was with a 9 year old friend, David Roback who lived on Nob Road. The boys sped from the body and stopped an adult neighbor, R. Thomas Walker. The Utica Police were called and found Joanne's half-nude body lying face down with her wrists tied to a tree branch with black shoelaces and a length of rawhide bound around her neck. The knot was later identified as a "Granny," and taught to be used in Boot Camp by the Marine Corps. It was the same type knot the Troopers found on the rope found on Potato Hill sixteen months later near the grave of Mary Rose Turner. The Coroner, Dr. Brady said Joanne died about 3 p.m. and she had multiple stab wounds and was raped...Being tied to a tree was the second M.O. of rape in the Utica area.

A strange but morbid twist of fate occurred when the Utica Police were called to the scene by Mr. Walker. The day watch commander of the criminal division was Joanne's uncle, Lt. Ray Pecheone. He was one of the first officers to arrive and had to be led from the crime scene by fellow officers sobbing and devastated by what he saw. Thirty six years later a reward of $12,000. lays in the account of the "Night Stick Club" a civilian group who are police friendly, awaiting the arrest and conviction of Joanne's murderer. The only description rendered by people in the area was distributed by the police as, "White male, in his 20's, 5' 10", wearing a 3/4 length brown or green jacket and unlaced black boots. Many of the witnesses in the vicinity of the homicide said they saw a car parked at the foot of the path at about 3 p.m., described as a , "Late model, bronze or gold compact car . Prior to the Pecheone murder the Utica Police records room had only one unsolved murder, that was the case of Mrs. Lillian Mishalane, a 69 year old widow who was found brutally murdered near her home in West Utica, 2 blocks from Bohling's Shell Station. She was last seen roaming the streets early in the morning and suffering from insomnia.. Hatch was a free man at the time of this murder.

The stark report contained in the Utica Police Department files, indexed under," Missing Persons," recited, "September 8, 1971, Mrs. Victoria Penar (mother) reported Lorraine Penar Zincola missing from 1002 Sunset Avenue, Utica, N.Y. since July 9,1971 at about 8:30 a.m. Report received by Officer V.D. Colucci, assigned to the Juvenile Aid Division, Policewoman, M.L. Salmon. Zone cars alerted, teletype message, file 6) sent to area police agencies. Also, a teletype message sent to Albany requesting information pertaining to a vehicle registered to missing subjects. Officer Salmon stated, "Periodically spoke to mother and husband of missing woman; a separation or divorce in progress, and spoke to Attorney Smith. Mother and children left to go on a vacation before school started. Age (mother) 26, 5' 5" 125 lbs, blue eyes, brown hair. 1961 Olds, green 4 door, N.Y. Reg. 8542 UZ. Reason for leaving home: went on vacation with three sons, Joseph 7, James 4, Mark 2."

There was nothing to make the grandmother anxious or curious as she kissed her daughter and three grandsons and waved to them as they drove away on July 9, 1971.

She never suspected it would be the last tie she saw them. It was a month later when she opened her daughter's reconciliation statement from the First Federal Savings and Loan that she had withdrawn $4,000.00 the day before she left, July 8, 1971. A few days before her vacation trip she had shared an intimacy with a bowling friend, Lorraine Vennero, that she was "Going South to marry a parolee by the name of Bernard Hatch .and he was going to 'jump' parole."

Asked by the Troopers why Mrs. Penar didn't report her missing grandchildren and daughter until two months later, her explanation was," I wondered why the children didn't start school after Labor Day." During the investigation after the Cady's were found, and unsure if it was a son and Mrs. Zinicola, the State Police followed the paper trail from the bank withdrawals the day before she left. David Winston, President of First Federal audited the transaction and found that Lorraine had requested and received $2,000.00 in cash and $2,000.00 in American Express Travelers Checks. The trail ended when the Manhattan State Police Investigator retrieved the cashed checks and they were endorsed and cashed in the Amsterdam Savings Bank, Amsterdam, N.Y. in the late morning of July, 9, 1971. Amsterdam is located 60 miles east of Lorraine's home in Utica. The State Police faced a hurdle when they realized there were no teller's stamp on the checks. Interviewing the employees of Amsterdam Savings, failed to reveal anyone who recalled the transaction. Linda Cady extracted $345.00 the day before she was missing and last seen.

Lorraine and her husband Joseph had begun divorce proceedings in November, 1970 and a final decree was granted on June 19, 1972 . Paradoxically, Joseph's attorney for the proceedings was Steve Pawlinga.

During the intensive search in December 1973 on Potato Hill,, charred children's clothing were found. After they were brought to Lorraine Zinicola's family for identification they were positively determined as those belonging to Lorraine and the boys. The car has never been found.

The defense attorney interview

Out of a sense of fairness and to balance the ledger I chose to interview the Defense Attorney for Hatch, Steven Pawlinga. We had exhausted the people from the prosecutors side, probation Officers, NYSP, Pathologist, Parole Officer, National Guardsmen, Judge, jurors and lay witnesses. Our purpose was to develop a "Level playing field." We discovered that Steve Pawlinga was not eager, nor enjoyed, any discussion about the Hatch trial. He would have been happier to review his victories. He represented Hatch twice and was batting 500.

Unannounced, I dropped into his office one morning, a violation of protocol for the law profession. After responding to the secretary's question concerning my purpose, no I was not a client, no, I didn't have an appointment,. She said he was at the County Court House doing research.

I caught up with him as he peered at the stacks of law cases. After exchanging amenities, I told him we were writing a book about Hatch. He already knew about our mission. He declined quickly as I asked if he'd be interested in writing a chapter or two.

He opened with, "It was a blue ribbon jury, highly intelligent. After all, what do you get when a trial lasts as long as Hatch's did? " I translated his remark by assuming the jury didn't win his prize for accomplishment, just different than what he was used to in Oneida County. I followed him to the McKinney's section and asked what I felt, was a nondescript question. "Did you ever see Hatch blink?" I was hopeful he'd validate what others had observed. His response was unhesitating, "No-come to think of it, I didn't. How about the others, Wolff, Judge Walsh, the jurors? I was closer, physically, to Bernard than anyone else." I answered, "We've interviewed a ton of people Steve: jurors, Judge Walsh, court attendants, the State Police who sat with Ted and they all agree,-he didn't blink. Odd, isn't it?"

His next statement surprised me, "You know, he came from a straight, middle class family, the type that don't show their emotions." My thought was that it was a simple solution to a complex problem. I wondered how you correlate an unconditioned reflex to sociology.

He jumped to the trial when he said, "I'd win that case today with the new laws and forensic advances, DNA and the other sophisticated stuff that find people innocent." He continued, "Did you read the transcript, couple of thousand pages? Probably not. Don't you think I was on the money during the cross of the chemical evidence?" He never waited for an answer and thought it flippant if I told him I was there for most of the trial and reacted with a nod.

Steve assumed an immodest stature as he said, "I was a science major at Colgate, pre-med, so I had an advantage when we got into the forensic stuff, the lab guys from the State Police were stammering during my cross. Ted was OK but didn't have my background. You read the testimony, you'll know what I'm talking about."

He walked toward one of the chairs next to the elongated mahogany table, removing his suit jacket and straightening the shoulders to avoid wrinkles and without provocation he said, "And Nowak, that lying bastard, he's the one that did me in." Despite being a convicted felon, Nowak's surprise testimony when he was

Hatch's cellmate, passed the credibility test with the jury. I realized that Steve didn't take the life conviction lightly.

He continued with his rancor about Nowak. "I was had by that son-of-a-bitch." I knew he was still on the Nowak kick. Reverting back to the sociologic profile and the blinking absence he said, " You know Tom, his mother is tough too. She's the type that never shows any emotion, still alive in her nineties. Can you believe that? " He knew she was alive as Hatch's mother had quitclaimed the deed to Pawlinga for her camp in Forestport to pay for an appeal that he lost The foundation for requesting a reversal was a rather ingenious statement framed as a question when Hatch took the stand. Ted asked, as the final barrage, "Isn't it unusual Mr. Hatch that many of your acquaintances end up dead or missing? Judge Walsh disallowed it and had the question stricken. The Appellate Court did not reverse the conviction and said it didn't merit reversal.

Processing my invitation to contribute a couple of chapters from the defense side, he said, "Publishers are after me about writing a book about Hatch, really the trial. Didn't have time, became the mayor of Utica and all that goes with it. They thought I'd be a special author because of my forensic, chemical knowledge. As I think about it, maybe I should have gone to Med School."

I never broached the prospect of having a standard question and answer session with him since he seemed more open and comfortable in the Law Library, walking to the stacks and taking a book and scribbling citations in his yellow pad.

The cross examination by Attorney Pawlinga of one of the chemists from the State Police Lab included the declaratory statement that he was a pre-med student at Colgate University. Maybe it was a warning that the chemist better be on his toes. I recall his words, "That's why I'm able to ask you such searching, scientific and technical questions." I remember the response from the veteran testifier who had spent more time in the witness chair than Pawlinga had spent in a barber's chair. He said, "Yes sir Counselor, I've heard you are able and well schooled in the profession." The "Blue Ribbon Jury" wasn't impressed, neither was the chemist.

Steve appeared to relish our dialogue as he continued, "Strictly circumstantial, strictly and absolutely. Today I'd get him off." There was a degree of certitude as he said it. I left with the impression that the words, "Getting him off," did not mean innocent but maybe a hung jury and another trial.

"I've got the testimony in my office if you're bent on reading it, thousands of pages." I thanked him for his time and told him we have access to the transcript at the records room of the courthouse.

With a hint of sincerity, but more to stroke his ego I said, "Your students, the cops who had you in class, still remember you as the teacher who made them memorize the fourth amendment and you made them spit it back, verbatim, no notes." Grinning he asked, "How do you know that?" My response was, "Every time I mention your name they say, "Yeah, the 4th amendment lawyer." Steve grinned with a sense of contentment.

The thin, bespectacled lady who enjoys the title of "Reference person," interrupts us. The timing was perfect as the intense researchers were glancing at us out of the corner of their eye. They were about to tell us to quiet down. I recalled the framed portrait of Abraham Lincoln that says, "A lawyer's time and advice is his stock in trade."

My parting words were, "I see Hatch's daughter got jammed up." His unnerving retort was, "Yeah, she's crazy too." I didn't read anything into the statement but later surmised he felt Hatch was pathological. We exchanged cards and he said, "Call me if you want to read the transcript." He didn't accept my extended arm to shake his hand but I looked in his eyes as he blinked a number of times

Cassandra, the student and the casualty

Hatch left more sufferers than the families of his victims. His only daughter was one. Every criminal leaves a legacy and it's almost always ugly. The commentary of Hatch's daughter will be summarized by the last paragraph, her obituary.

Cassie or Cassy, as her nickname was spelled by different people, started her college in March of 1979. Her high school transcript caused her to be placed in the "Full Opportunity Program" a euphemism for, "Needs some help." Community Colleges have an open door policy, meaning, they'll give everyone a chance to rise or fall. Cassy took remedial courses and then left after a semester. She regained her vision in the Spring of 1984 and enrolled in the Criminal Justice Program. With her father doing a life sentence, twenty six years of age and a single Mom, her future was bleak.

She took a bus to the college for her preliminary visit, her grandmother cared for her diapered son. She greeted the counselor with an immediate question, "Can I take Criminal Justice and become a guard if my Dad is doing time?" Shocked but not ruffled, Ms. Berlin gave an indirect reply, "I'm not quite sure. Let me call the C.J. Department, they'll know."

The professor's response to the question was followed by a question. "What does she want to do, help him escape?" He continued with, "I guess she could, but would never be allowed to work in the same facility." Covering the speaker end with her hand, she said to Cassy, "Probably- he'll help you with your schedule.". Upon hearing the professors name, Cassy said ,"He knows my Dad, he was at his trial often."

Cassy and the professor had their first formal meeting. She said, after a hand shake, "You know my Dad, I know you do. His name is Bernard Hatch." The reply was curt, "Yes-kind of. How's he doing?" She never answered. Her name was Snyder, not Hatch and he wasn't certain the background check would pick up on her maiden name. "We'll talk again at registration, the 21st to the 25th.".

106

It was no surprise when she chose the courses that were directed towards her father's incarceration: Probation, Pardon and Parole, Corrections Administration, Criminology and Abnormal Psychology. She became a sterling student, participating in classroom discussions, sought extra help, turned her papers in early and often came to his office to visit about her father. She had street savvy and the students listened with awe as she'd repeat incidences.

One day after class she came to the professor and wanted to know the details of her father's sentence, earliest release date, credit for time served and parole board decision making. She took notes as the process was related: " I hear he's a model prisoner, does his own time, private, no tickets, no bad time, lifts a lot and has had only one fight. The Board looks at the population, empty beds, society, pre-sentence report, victim's family and their attitude, the sentencing judge, the D.A. Lots of elements. His first review will be 1997 and they, the Board,, are reluctant to release on the first go around." She didn't seem happy with his comments as they painted a grim picture.

Sergeant Roman was retired at the time, called a medical disability. He was a local magistrate in New York Mills, N.Y. He was also a guest speaker at the college, recounting the Hatch murder to the attentive students. She said, "I want to talk directly, eyeball to eyeball, to Judge Roman and get some answers. Do you think he'll tell me whether my Dad should be roaming the streets?"

The professor hedged his answer. "I don't know Cassy, he'll tell you as much as you want to know. A lot of it will be surmise, hunches, attitude. You have to remember, he was a cop, I'm a theoretician. When you work a case, look for bodies, arresting people, making next of kin announcements ,it's a different ball game. Maynard and I disagree on the death penalty, but we are coming from different perspectives. He's been in the trenches, I've been an onlooker." A meeting was agreed upon.

Maynard was unduly polite during the interview, sharing as much information as he could, answering her pointed questions and not encroaching on her relationship with her father. Maynard quickly realized she was trying to come to grips with her torn allegiance and her innate desire to have him released, whenever. Her reaction became evident in the next paper submitted, as she proclaimed "the importance of societal protective rights and safeguards against predators."

Cassy was fourteen when her father was sentenced. She was a floor below the court room during her father's trial, in Family Court, represented by a Law Guardian, for what she called, "Grand Theft Auto." Her adjudication as a Juvenile Offender would be sealed, protected from others, exclusive of law enforcement and the courts.

Maynard was able to extract some personal data when she said, "Dad weighs 220, I had to tell him when he hugged me, take it easy, the last time I visited him. Not an ounce of fat, 30" waist. His neck is as big as my thigh. He stopped smoking, went from three packs a day to none." Her course in abnormal psych seemed to give her the starting point for an explanation of his terrorism. It was perceptible that she had been gored by the horns of a dilemma. She spoke of her Grandfather Hatch burning her dad's fingers, putting him on a horse, alone when he was two, telling him that boys don't kiss men, encouraging Bernie to shoot a cow. She was trying to deliver a point that Roman wouldn't be normal if that was his background.

She called her mother's suicide, an overdose and her Grandfather Rooney's death on the railroad tracks, an accident. She became assertive when she attempted to get Sergeant Roman to justify police tactics as she relived her father's arrest. "I was with Dad the night they arrested him. Maybe you were there, Judge. I swear to God, they wanted to kill him, holding and cocking their guns, 357's. I was on the floor of the back seat, October 17, 1973. It seems like yesterday. I'd love to see his pre-sentence report, the psychological report. Maybe they would help me understand why I am like I am. Genes stay with you." For whatever reason she told Maynard about she and her dad double dating with the Snyder's, he with the older sister, she with her deceased spouse, the younger brother. "Odd wasn't it, Snyder-Snyder, Hatch-Hatch. Try that one on for size, Judge!"

She suddenly took a strange tack when she asked, "Did you ever hear that Linda was pregnant before she went missing?" Not waiting for a reaction, she tried to repudiate it, by claiming, "Dad always said Mom was the only one who would get his seed. He was extra careful, he never believed girls when they said they were safe, he was super careful. I knew Dad." Maynard wondered, why that declaration?

It was the third week of the semester, a warm day for late February in Upstate, New York, high 50's. As the professor walked between aisles, trying to stir a discussion from the class, he walked by Cassy who had a tank top on. Baring her left outer forearm he eyed an unprofessional tattoo, inscribed was "Dad," in script. She had obviously wanted it displayed and he asked, pointing to it, "Where did you get that, Sylvan Beach?" The answer was terse, "No, some guy did it. Lousy job, huh?" His immediate thought was whether any of his three daughters would have "Dad" displayed on their arm. He rejected the possibility

During one of the later discussions he opened with, "You knew your father had a fixed gaze, some say he didn't blink .Is that plausible?" Cassy looked at the library books on the chair next to her, all abnormal psych texts, trying obviously to unravel or understand her dysfunction, she replied, "I don't think he was two personalities, maybe more, multiple. Do you?" He said, "I don't have a clue, that's out of my discipline." Her next question was startling and unanswerable. "I heard from someone that Mary Rose was my grandmother Hatch, a throwback from when she nursed him until he was five, Linda and Lisa were my mother and me and the Zinicola kids were the Smith kids (my step-brothers). Do you believe that?" The professor bent over in his chair and placed his right hand over his brow as if in thought. His answer was, "I don't have the foggiest."

"Here's another puzzler, put this in your book too. My Aunt Victoria had a baby after the Cady's were missing. Guess what she called her?" Never waiting for the answer, she raised her voice and said, "Lisa Ann! She's about thirteen now, probably doesn't have any idea who she was named after."

To balance the aforementioned with the chapter title, it becomes evident that Cassandra was a victim, also.

The spring semester of the following year, Cassy stopped going to class. Her transcript showed two "F's" and two "NG's" . She disconnected with the professor and on March, 26, 1985, he received, from the Application Investigation Unit, Department of Correctional Services, a covering letter and forms, requesting Cassy's school records and any pertinent comments from former teachers. She had signed an authorization releasing the information. They wanted to know her character traits, dependability, cooperation, courtesy and appearance, with an explanation. They also asked for, "Any confidential information on file and if there is, please elaborate below or if you prefer to have the Investigator contact you personally, please indicate below."

The letter and the attachments left the professor open-mouthed and dazed. His gut reaction was to call Cassy and get her consent or refusal to share his information about her father, if they weren't already privy to his background. He was gored by the dilemma and it was uncomfortable. He breathed a sigh of relief when she told him to forget it, she was enmeshed in too many personal problems, couldn't leave her son if she was accepted and seemed completely unglued and said, "I have no future, especially in the criminal justice system." She was distraught. The professor had his anxiety diminished.

Her obituary was standard reading for those who were not understanding nor knowledgeable, of her life and misfortunes. It read, " Cassandra Helene Snyder, 45, Munnsville, died June 18, 2005, at her home, following a courageous battle with cancer. She was born on February, 22, 1960 in Herkimer, the daughter of Andrea Rooney Smith. Cassandra lived in Utica most of her life. She was a 1976 graduate of Utica Free Academy, later attending Mohawk Valley Community College. She has lived in Munnsville the past 15 years. She had been a volunteer for Victims of Violence, and enjoyed reading, writing and spending time with family and friends." The survivors are omitted by the writer.

The name Hatch was never included, her father was never mentioned.

Cassandra

The reader will determine what is vital to the story. Cassie's interview was initiated by her and she agreed to have it recorded. Notes were taken and compared for transcription. The tape was played over and over, stopped, started, making certain the words were carefully transcribed. This resulted in the production of the dialogue of August 17, 1993. The diary was copied with her permission.:.

"I was reintroduced to my father in December 1970. I knew he was implicated in the Pecheone murder that was never solved. I knew the knots were similar to Navy, Marine knots. It was a ritualistic murder ,as I recall, but Dad had an alibi. Dad and Bohling used to snowmobile in the area. Dad used to test drive cars after he worked on them. Will the book affect his parole? Will the parole board know he was implicated in the Cady and Zinicola murders?

Are you afraid of your father?

No, not at all! He should be afraid of me ,at this point. And I'm serious, and I don't mean that in a threatening manner. I don't mean I'd never kill or dismember him in any way, shape or form. No, I'm not afraid of him, he should be afraid of me for what he put my mother through, my grandmother through.

Your grandmother told me she slapped him one time.

Oh yeah, she did, because I came in with a slap mark on my face. He had slapped me. He laughed when she did that, he laughed. I even have notes from when I was living up there with him, in Steuben. and I was homesick and I wanted to come back home, desperately, and it was Easter Sunday that he agreed to take me to Utica and let me go to church with my mother, my grandmother and the kids. I was just living through everything the other day and I was getting out suicide notes and all kinds of things.

Your suicide notes?

No, my mothers.

She left notes?

Oh yes!

I also have her diary, but there's, not really, not too much in that. The majority of everything else burned down. I had everything in storage in my step-parents barn that burned down a year and a half ago. So I lost my paper work. It killed me. I came across the one note. He used to write me notes when I was on the phone with my mother and grandmother-tell them this-tell them that. He'd program me as to what exactly to say. He wrote me this note, "Please Cassandra , you have to promise me that you won't say anything about being homesick, you have to come back, I'll pick you up. I don't want them keeping you,"-this, that and the other thing He made me write a letter to my step-father saying I wanted my real father and mother back together again-he dictated this fourteen page letter.

How did you get along with your step-father?

No response

Didn't you get stopped by the parole officer one time?

We got pulled over by the police. He got a ticket for failure to keep right.

I remember that. You were in the car.

I was driving. I went a little too far to the left, the cop was coming toward us when the cop turned around we switched seats. I was 13 at the time, 13. He used to do little things to rekindle the father- daughter relationship and secure my trust in him, which was to be expected under the circumstances. He didn't want me to turn on him, I guess. I can't believe I went up there to Steuben, the beginning of the winter, and in April he's committing murders. He just got his daughter back after all those years and us not having a relationship . This is what he could have been doing?

You were living with the Pulcini's at the time?

Yeah, I had spent Christmas at home, New Years, and I believe I went there right before my thirteenth birthday, February 22nd. Was it problematical? Of course it was. I hated the fact my father was there.. There were things that happened. I was resentful, very resentful.

Your mother was married to Mr. Smith at the time?

Yes, but they had been separated for many years, but they were attempting a reconciliation, but of course, my father was always there to step in the middle of that. Meanwhile, he was having affairs with numerous women, but he doesn't want my mother to have a life. He wanted to dictate everybody's moves.

Earliest recollections. Had you picked up a snake so you wouldn't be afraid of snakes, at your father's command? Wasn't it in the driveway at Parris Island?

That was a different time, it was in the woods.

Are you afraid of snakes today?

No. I had a five and a half foot Boa Constrictor. I was petrified for many years, then I used to sleep with the Boa.

Do you remember living in Parris Island?

Oh yeah! I remember lying on the rocks in the driveway. I used to have excruciating stomach aches. I was homesick, I missed my momma. My momma told me that when I went down there I was potty trained for quite some time and I started to mess my pants, so I was having some sort of psychological reaction to the move, or whatever. I was there late '62-'63. I can definitely remember. I used to take my shoes-we lived in a trailer park, and the kids down there didn't wear shoes. I assumed they were poor and couldn't afford shoes. The first week we were there I went through ten pairs of shoes. I used to take mine off and give them to the kids. I remember the swing set. I remember

Your father was on pass or leave .from Parris Island when he was arrested on the first rape case.?

Yeah, we lived on Holland Avenue.

Do you remember anything about that incident?

No, other than what I read or what have you.. We were separated from my father at the time. I remember leaving one night with Bill Smith, which was supposedly why my father, why my father went on to do that or whatever. He came home for my mother and we had left and went up to Munnsville and so he freaked out, and, you know, it sent him on a tangent. I was born on February, '60, and that was '64. I believe, late November '63? Sentenced in '64. Mother and Bill married in '65. So I didn't know about that 'till I was 10 years old, when I came across the newspaper article-that was my first knowledge. I was too young, I wouldn't have known about that.

Do you think we could produce this delicately enough without making any accusations-let people,-the readers, surmise or draw inferences?

Well,-are we going to introduce the Cady's, the Zinicola's ,and other things?

Yes, we'll have to separate chapters-Cady-Zinicola. We've interviewed all the Cady's friends and relatives.

Do you recall the circumstance when your Grandfather Hatch came down and he had a dog with him?

And he made my father kill the dog?

And there was another circumstance. This was when your father wrenched the heads off of the puppies.

No. I heard that. My grandfather made my father shoot the puppy. I even had a picture of my dad when he was two years old with his arms around the dogs.

I'm not sure, but I don't know whether the dog got into the meal-there was a bucket of meal and your Grandfather Hatch either directed him-he was 7 or 8 at the time, to either shoot the dog or Grandfather

Hatch shot the dog. Another weird thing. Did your Grandfather and Grandmother Hatch go on their honeymoon with one of the parents?

No, it was my mother and father. When my father was driving the car at the time, Grandma Hatch was sitting in the back and he had to drive with one hand and hold his mother's hand in the back seat. I have a lot of pictures.

To get back to the Cady's and Zinicola's, you probably know about the joint savings account that Mrs. Penar, Lorraine's mother, had with Lorraine. They had a joint savings account at Cornhill Savings and Loan, and the last day they were seen alive, she left with the three kids and she withdrew, I think, four thousand dollars, and got a cashiers check.. Drove to Amsterdam, 62 miles east , stopped in a bank in Amsterdam, cashed the check for the four thousand and they've never been seen since.

I know my mother was always curious as to where he was getting his cars from and had an Oldsmobile 442 and he came one week to the house with this convertible and it was painted red. About a month later he came with a black convertible which was, in fact, the same car and he had it painted. My mother said, "What do you think I am-stupid. It's the same car and you had it painted." "No it's not, it's a different car." She said, "Bah, it's the same car." Well, one of my barrettes had fallen out and it was under the seat in the back. My mother said, "Where did Cassandra's barrette come from, what do you think I am-stupid?" He only worked for minimum wage and he would come up with these four or five thousand dollar cars. Where the hell was he getting them from? My mother was a little investigative reporter in her own right and she used to follow him around and I even spoke with the Zinicola kids.

Did you?

Oh yeah. She dropped me off one day and I went around the corner and talked to little Joey and I'd call the house on occasion when the kids weren't in school and I lied and said I was a classmate and why he wasn't in school and my mother kept a watch on him. She knew a lot of his goings-on. She was very suspicious of him.

When he raped that little girl in Ilion--------

See, I didn't know it was a rape. The paper said abduction.

It was abduction and rape. The affect of the appeal was a question of jurisdiction between Oneida and Herkimer Counties and brought her to Oneida County.

And then dropped her back off at her home?

Within a block of her home, yes.

But to get back to him cleansing himself with milkweed, he had this compulsion about being clean. I know this man, he would take two or three showers a day. Oh yeah!

Which is kind of an obsessive-compulsive personality. But you'd never know he was a mechanic by looking at his fingers.

Oh no. That was the strangest thing about him. He'd change a transmission or a motor and he'd have to go wash his hands. He had long nails too.

Did he?

Not long-long, but for a man. I don't know whether my grandmother told you or not, but that afternoon when she called the house, my father was in the bathroom throwing up. He was very sick. He even got a bottle of ginger brandy to calm his stomach.

What date was that?

When Mary Rose was last seen.

When Mary Rose was last seen?

The twenty seventh.

The twenty seventh?

Mama remembered that well because she called on the phone and I said, "He's in the bathroom," and she said, "What's wrong with him?" and I said, "He's throwing up"

That was Thursday. Did you go to school that day?

I don't know whether there was school. Maybe we were off for spring or Easter vacation, or maybe it was after school, because I'd get home about 2:30

Holland Patent or Remsen?

Holland Patent. Check the records to see if I was on vacation. I don't know whether there was school going on or not.

When was the first time you saw him that day?

I'm trying to remember that too. The Pulcini's said it was about 11:00. It seems as though I was home.

115

Then they executed the search warrant on Monday. Do you remember that vividly?

Oh yeah. Oh God yeah.

It was kind of scary wasn't it? Because I think your grandmother Hatch was very protective of you. I think the BCI wanted to talk to you separately.

They never wanted me to be alone with anyone. Once I voluntarily went to Marcy to the juvenile unit on an out-patient basis. I used to go once a week. I demanded that I went after my father got arrested and all, because I was having some problems with kids at school, serious problems and just having a hard time coping with everything and they would constantly pump me-never to mention anything about the shovel-never to mention anything about ever being in the area. My father would never understand why I ever went to a "Shrink." He was dead-set against me talking to anyone. Oh yes, John and Victoria didn't want me to either. I said,- "Listen! .I need to talk to someone-,somebody. I need help! I'm going to go insane " .I was sitting on the bed, pulling my hair out. You know, just beside myself. Of course, I never divulged anything in regard to that , I just talked about the problems I was having at school.-the different fights I was having and I was in the bathroom, in the stall, and I'd hear, "Oh-yeah. That Hatch has murderer's blood in her veins. You know what her father did?" It was really hard to deal with, I had a lot of fights.

Of course, whatever you said to the psychiatrist would be privileged anyway.

Of course-of course.

They didn't understand that?

They are psychiatrist-shy. They really are. I've gone over the years a number of times-after the episode with Cavoli-after the death of my husband- a lot of the times when I felt the need. The mind is just like every other body part-if you get sick-go to a doctor and get it fixed,-you know. They don't think that way. They're very-----it makes me wonder why they're afraid to let a person get in their mind. What's so secretive? What's there to hide? That someone is going to get inside your mind and discover your inner thoughts? Personally, I don't care-you know-about my inner thoughts. The last time I went to see my father, I don't know whether you knew my friend Dave Galono, but he came with me.

That was in Clinton (Dannemora prison)?

Yeah, and I went to the bathroom and to get refreshments from the vending machine and after we left, Dave told me that my father said to him, "You know Cassy has a lot of problems and she's been to a psychiatrist before." I don't know whether he said that for fear I'd divulge some secret to Dave or forewarning him not to take me seriously because I have a few screws loose. I mean he has a problem with that and I heard he hasn't been to one all these years. He's underwent no therapy-so you know-I wasn't aware he ever had a psychiatric evaluation.

Well, Dr. Bigelow never interviewed him.

I don't think so.

There s a psychiatric evaluation from Attica. Remember when he did his first seven years or so? They found him fairly normal.

Huh! Serial killers. You often hear the neighbors , "This guy was the nicest guy." In his spare time he was devouring intestines in the living room with Grey Poupon.. You know, I mean it's common-Jeffrey Darmer. I don't know. Who's to know. When you can detach reality like that and then just go back. I don't know. Who's to know?

What do you remember about the search?

At the trailer?

Yes

Everything. Just about everything.

Tom Gallagher-Tom Carl?

I remember them. I remember the bald headed gentleman getting stung by a bee.

Is that right? I wonder who that was?

He went over by the dog's pen and I said to him, "Better not stick your hand in there., you might get bit."

You were kind of walking around with them?

Oh yeah-oh yeah.. It was a sickening sight. They were sarcastic. I mean they tipped my father's room upside down and they put out a butt of a cigar on the mattress. The whole road was full of cops cars. You'd think they were coming for a regimental army instead of one man.

But your father wasn't there when they first arrive, was he?

No, he didn't show up until 4 o'clock. They made him stand naked for three or four hours. I had my period and they went through the garbage-opened up sanitary pads-went through all the cupboards-dumped all the food out. They checked everything. They found some newspaper articles about the murder in the dresser drawer. It may have been because it happened in the neighborhood. Then the week before they were rummaging through the garbage. That's when Nowak was supposedly the garbage truck operator, or what have you.

No, Nowak was lifting weights with your father while in the Oneida County Jail.

.Oh-OK. I heard something about him working for the garbage company up there.. I believe I'm correct.

Nowak was working for the Town of Steuben?

Yes, if I'm not mistaken.

The trial indicated that he was lifting weights.

At the time? At the time? Of course, Nowak isn't too believable... He has a history of lying.

Then there was a strong constitutional question. The courts have since ruled that when you put garbage out, it becomes public domain-you've relinquished any expectation of privacy. Your Uncle John came out and screamed at the troopers. It's intrusive, don't you think?

No, not really. Especially if there's a murder investigation going on. Hey! What do people put in their garbage that they'd be afraid of someone going through it? Personal? The police can come and go though my garbage any day of the week. I don't care. More power to them.

I think the best way to approach this is-do you have a tape recorder at home?

Yeah. I have a teeny-tiny one. Pocket one. I'm not sure, maybe an over-skeptic?

I don't blame you. You have had a lot of people disappoint you in your life. Do you want to address it so you can go back, historically, and relate what might be important, on a tape, or do you want to outline it?

What's a cul-de-sac?\

It's a turnaround, circular driveway, sort of.

How far after Weaver saw him dragging the body did he report it and was the area searched? Was it a matter of days?

Weaver is a principal subject of our book, so far.

Is he still alive?

Weaver's still alive. He's not very old-46 47 now. I spent almost a full day with Weaver.. He saw the body going by, about 10-1030 in the morning, drove to Boonville, went to Agway and he wanted to pick up some gasoline and fill the tractor he borrowed before he returned it. So, he talked to the guys in Agway and told them what he saw. They told him that maybe he should call the State Police. James has a brother that was a little "Funny," and James is a little "Funny" too . So, he started to call the State Police about 1;30. They, Trooper Chaffee, didn't show up until about 7:00 o'clock that night.

And when was that, April 27th?

Yes. Thursday the 27th.

Yes

My father always wanted me to reunite with him,, allow me to do whatever wrong I wanted to do, to ingratiate himself with me. It was as simple as that, you know, At that time I thought it was cool.

Was your mother strict?

Oh yeah-extremely strict and very worried that something similar that happened to her would happen to her daughter , that was her bi. That's why she sent me up there to live with him. Little did she know he was doing everything in his power to see to it that----------A lot of sexual connotations, yeah.

With him?. .

Yeah. He tried to french kiss me one night and he also told me one night that if I ever decided to have sex that I should come to him first because he would be gentle and kind and understanding to me, whereas a young boy would just want to "have his way" with me.

How old were you then?

I was thirteen. It made me very uncomfortable and nervous-very nervous. But I was far from being ready to have sex to start out with, and certainly not with my own father-and he didn't force himself on me-I mean it was a very uncomfortable conversation –but it's not like he wanted to "have his way" with me- he was just feeling me out. He wanted to know how sexually educated I was. I remember he asked me if I knew what an orgasm was and I said I didn't , but I didn't want to say no and sound stupid and I said "yeah, I do." And he said, "can you explain it to me?" I said, "I know what it is but I don't know how to explain it." I'll never forget it because I didn't have the slightest idea what an orgasm was. I didn't know what the hell he was talking about. But now look back on those conversations and stuff, I realize just how sick they were and would probably happen if I were a willing participant.

Had he talked about his other exploits with other women?

I used to watch out the window for him. I was his lookout. He'd go in the bedroom with Rose Mary Snyder and I'd have to go sit in the kitchen and watch for my aunt and uncle-oh yeah.

In the trailer?

Yeah!

(Glancing through the diary) This diary is fascinating.

I wish there were more. I wish she had written everything she had found out.

June 18th, saw Bob and Zinicola in a black car.

Is this really true that he slashed his wrists?

I doubt it.

He told me he got his wrist caught as you go to the visiting area there. When you hear the door slam and it locks in your face and he got his hand caught.

I think it was just sensationalism.

See. That's what gets me the most and I'm never going to know who lied and who told the truth. I know the lies my relatives told to a certain degree on things that I was there for and I know they were deliberate lies-we'll never know who lied and who told the truth-beyond a shadow of a doubt. That's Lisa Ann and Linda's bodies? (looking at photos). There's no way they could have lied or falsified that information.

You mean the autopsy report?

Yes.

I don't know. This guy in Syracuse, this medical examiner. He's been under the gun.

They must have lied. I was too young to have remembered that. Then Mrs. Hinman passed away and she was good friends with her daughter, Dorothy Hinman, and they used to go out to dinner every

Wednesday night-it was a constant friendship sort of thing, and she stayed on to take care of the house a few years after Mrs. Hinman died.

But that was the house she owned?

No, but she didn't stay at Soule Road then.

So she didn't stay at Soule Road then?

Yes, that's when she stopped taking care of Hinman's . I'm not sure if she and Dorothy had a falling out or what happened but she decided to buy the trailer and move in with my aunt and uncle and that was when she left there. So, that must have been '93 when she bought that trailer.

When they executed the search warrant at the trailer they didn't find certain things. They didn't find the tires. Investigator Peo went to Deansboro-looked in the garage window and saw some tires in there and they executed the second warrant after the trailer search.

And they were his tires?

Yes, they were his tires.

OK. John Pulcini would be the link to that, I'm sure. My grandmother wouldn't take the tires up there-you know!

Do you think your grandmother had access to that house? Hinman's?

Yes. Yeah-she did.

But she didn't live there-she was living in the trailer at the time.

No. Like I said, it had to be June or July,'73, that she got that trailer 'cause they had to dig for the septic tank and the whole 9 yards. They couldn't have done that in April or March-so she was still up there.

At Hinman's during the week and weekends?

She'd stay during the week and on weekends she'd go to Forestport.. She must have gotten that in the summer of '73 because I was living right next door at Victoria's and John's. I remember them putting in the platform and getting the trailer, so it must have come out after my father-you know—through the investigation and what not.

But your grandmother testified that she was home and Bernie went to bed at 9:30 in the morning.

Yeah-he also called in and said grandma was sick and he couldn't go to work. The fact was he was throwing up in the bathroom when my grandmother called. They're all liars. I wish to hell I could remember what time.

But I think he said he stayed at your grandmother's house in Deansboro. That's why they executed the search warrant.

No he did not! That was a deliberate lie-a deliberate, God dam lie. To the best of my knowledge my father never spent a night in Hinman's..

You think he came down Saturday night?

I know he did.

And did he go back to Forestport the next morning?

No. Went back that night.

Friday night?

Yes. I think I probably had school because we came back late Sunday night so my father wouldn't be observed sneaking out of the car and I probably had to go to school the next morning. And I do remember getting razzed by everyone on the school bus, and I got ticked off one day and I hit this kid in the head with my books.

Were you tough as a kid?

Oh yeah. I was very tough. I'd go in my room and cry. I was a pretty good fighter.

So you think you went to school Monday then?

I'm pretty sure-pretty sure.

I think it was Monday when the search warrant was executed.

That's right. I'm trying to remember. I did ride the school bus that day. I remember coming up the road and seeing an unmarked car, way down the end of our road at 365 and I can remember seeing another one at the next intersection and thinking. I can't remember whether I was on a dam school bus or whether my aunt or grandmother picked me up or what the heck.

But, if you were with your aunt or grandmother wouldn't you have had a conversation such as, "Oh-there's an unmarked car, I wonder what they're doing here?"

That's why I tend to think I was on the school bus.

You got off the school bus and went inside and John and Victoria were there and so was your grandmother?

The police weren't there yet, though they were watching from the road for my father-from every point -and I would .have had a conversation if I was with someone else. I did have a feeling about this. The process of elimination-I must have been on the school bus.

Do you think your grandmother drove down from Forestport by herself?

No. We drove down with my grandmother that Sunday night. I don't recall if he stayed at the trailer or not. I think he snuck in the trailer and went to work the next morning.

He went to work for Rintrona?

Yeah.-yeah.

He didn't require much sleep, did he?

No-no. Sometimes work right up until 9 and when the weather was good, he'd work 9-9:30 and "boom" then go to Bohlimg Shell at 11. But I'll try to think of his name----Oh, I wish I had kept a diary. Like I said, at that time I had complete faith in my father. I just thought he was getting framed.

Tell me about the school bus ride to the trailer.

Well-lets see. We got home at 2:35 or 2:40 and I was home by 5 after 3. It was between 20 to 25 minutes, depending on the weather.

How long were you home before the police arrived at the trailer door?

I'm trying to think-they came first, before dad arrived. He didn't show up until after 4:00 o'clock. He had an appointment with the parole officer that day. I'd say shortly after, Blanch. I got home between 3 and five after.

Shortly after you got home?

What does the report say?

They estimated it around 3 o'clock.

OK. So it was shortly after that I got there.

You were there when they rapped on the door?

Yes-yes.

Were you in the trailer?

Right opposite the trailer door. When they opened the door my bedroom was opposite the trailer door. The front door.

OK. A whole bunch of troopers?

There was a lot of people there.

And you kind of followed them around?

Oh yeah. I was talking.

Were you?

Yeah.

Did you hear the conversation between John Pulcini and the troopers?

My grandmother Hatch is a hysterical Annie and Victoria is an Annie too, and John is trying to be his tough guy self and so they were

Out and out. The cops were trying to be good and they said they had a warrant-search and seizure. They asked where my father was.

They took your father in the bedroom and stripped him? So you didn't see your father stripped?

No, but they had him there for a good long time. I'd say-3-3 ½ hours when------they kept him for a good long time. They made sure I was here and there. Yeah.

What was his reaction after the troopers left, after the search was finished. After the evidence was bagged and tagged?

I have no recollection.

Was he sad or mad?

He was mad because he had to stand there naked and they made fun of him having a "Big one." Or whatever.

TRANSFERENCE OF WORDS FROM THE DIARY- 1971

Birthdays: Marc- 3/12. Missy-1/15: Cassie-2/22:Gordie-2/23:Bob-3/5, Anniversary 10/31

2/11: Bob got a new car, '68 Olds convertible 442. Red outside, all black inside.

2/15: Bob bought 8 red roses for Valentines Day, didn't see him yesterday or hear from him.

2/18: Went on snowmobile with Bob to Frankfort. Howard, Betty and another man went too. It was wonderful, had a good time. Stopped at the Gardens.

2/22: Cassie's birthday. We had a party. 15 girls, Josephine and Paul Cioci, Ann, Cal. I took Cassie to see Mrs. Hatch. She's still in bed. Johnny, Bob's cousin came over. I didn't even think he remembered me.

2/23: Bob got a room to stay in the Lincoln Grille today.

2/29: Gordie Van Etten called here today after almost 4 years. He asked me to go out tonight. We went to see Liz Taylor and Warren Beatty in, "The only game in town." Then we went to White's in Chadwicks. I had my first Black Russian drink. We drove around afterwards and talked about everything. He's divorced from his second wife.

3/1: Gordie came over at 2:45 until 4:00 p.m. Brought my earring. I lost it in his car last night.. He left to go back to Vermont. We are going to write to each other again.

3/9: The telephone rang at 10:05 p.m. Someone was on it but didn't talk. It rang at 10:25 and the person said, "Who's this?" and we kept saying the same thing. I hung up. It rang again and it was Bob. He said hello "Andy" and we talked from 10:30 p.m. to 4:30 a.m. He kept telling me how much he loves me, always has and always will no matter what. First time we talked since he came home.

3/10: Marc's birthday-five years old. I picked Bob up at 1 p.m... at the gas station. We went to Kewpees, sat and talked to 1:45. He has a beard but he's going to take it off because I asked him to. He kept staring at me in the car and finally he grabbed me and kissed me. He said he wanted to do that the minute he got into the car. It was as if we had never been apart. It was the first time we had seen each other, face to face. Bob is supposed to call tonight. He's coming to supper on Friday. It will be Cassies first meeting with him since she was 2 years old. Bob and I talked last night from 10:30 to 12:35. We talked tonight until very late again.

3/12: Bob is supposed to see his parole office today. Met Bob at lunch time. We talked tonight from until 1:30 from 10:30.

3/13: Bob is supposed to come for dinner. Pick him up at 5:45. We went to the Boston Store. He bought a doll for Missy and a robot for Marc, two Barbie Dolls and a ring for Cassie. She was happy to see him. He took to the kids and they did to him, too. I talked to the parole officer today. Bob and I are very much in love, but we will always have obstacles in our way.

3/14: Had a birthday party for Marc, nine boys. Bob talked to Cassie for a minute this morning. He was supposed to go on a date today. I stayed up until 1:00 a.m. and then went to bed. I felt so bad about him being out. I just got into bed when the phone rang. It was Bob and we talked from 1:00 a.m. to 5:30 this morning. He said he was going to try to come here tomorrow.

3/15: Bob called at 1:30. Mother answered. When I came to the phone he said, "How's everything?" I said, "OK." He said, "I'll call you later," and hung up. I don't believe he'll be here. I think he has a date. He called me again at 3:00 p.m. and said to come and get me at the gas station. We all went for a ride and then came home. The kids watched Wizard of Oz. We ate supper. We left at 10:30 to take him home. We parked for awhile by his house. I got home at 1:15. Called him back and then went to bed.

3/16: Went to get estimates on my car. Stopped in the garage and gave Bob his cigarette case and gave him my old one, my silver one. He called me at 8:30. We talked a few minutes. He's going to call me back at 10.

3/17: St. Patrick's Day. Met Bob for lunch. We talked on the phone from 10:30 to 12:30.

3/18: Met Bob at 1:00. I said I was going to date so that we don't become too involved but he asked me not to, that he would take care of this other girl relationship, whatever it is. I wrote Gordie a letter about Bob and I.

3/19: Martin's birthday today.

3/20: Bob has a date tonight with some girl. I am trying to look at this in an adult manner. We are supposed to go for a fish fry today.

3/21: Cassie, Bob and I are supposed to go skating Saturday.

3/26: Was sitting in Bob's car in front of garage waiting for him. 11:30 p.m. a girl with long black hair came down Lincoln Ave. and turned up Court with Bob's '64 Olds. I wonder if she is his girl or if the crazy story he is handing me is true.

3/28: Bob came over after work .Mother went to church.

3/29: Bob and Cioci came at 10:00 p.m. on the bus. Bob stayed overnight. We made up the kids Easter baskets and did the eggs upstairs at Atter's. We all stayed up 'till 5:30 a.m. talking. Bob and I went shopping downtown for kids things.

3/30: We went to 12:30 mass. Bob left at 1:15. Regina and George came for dinner and then went to Julie's. I came home at 9:30 and the kids. The door bell rang and it was Bob. He helped me do all the dishes. I took him home at 1:30.

4/11: Bob and I went on a Girl Scout hike with Cassie. He gave Marc a bath, I gave Missy. He and I went to the Drive-In. We saw True Grit and Rose Mary's Baby. He peed in a cup at the Drive-In and how we laughed.

4/16: Bob came for supper. Cassie, he and I went to see Richard Burton in Ann of a thousand days. When I got home from taking him home, Mother said Victoria called. There was a Pontiac there. Also, Bill called at 11:30.Mom thought it was Bob and before he even said hello, she said, "What a good boy you are tonight. Next time I see you I have to pin a medal on you." Then he said hello and Helene hung up.

6/14: Bob, Mother, Missy and Marc and I went to Santa's North Pole up at Whiteface Mountain. It was the most beautiful----.

6/18: Saw Bob and Zinicola in the black car at 11:30 by her house. He must have stayed overnight.

6/20: Fathers Day. Bob, Cassie and I went to the St. Lawrence, Miller's Bay in Cape Vincent. We all swam in the St.L.

7/10: Friday. Lorraine Zinicola left Utica at 1:30. Bob started staying home steady. Black car was taken off the road.

Editors note: L. Zinicola and children were last seen on 7/9/71..

7/18: Bob and I went to Niagara Falls by ourselves. Went by Attica State Prison also. That was very depressing. The Falls was beautiful. We had a wonderful day. Too bad I can't get Zinicola out of my head. We could be very happy together now, but I can't ever trust him again.

7/28: Bob came with Olds 442 all painted black.

7/30: Red Olds convertible. Went to Oriskany Falls and had a drink. Wanted to buy me an anniversary present. I said no.

8/1:   Bob and I went up North, saw Dave and Susie. Stayed in Dayes in Forestport.

9/6: Bob and I, Victoria and Johnny went to the State Fair.

9/27: Monday. Mother went to talk to Mrs. Penar. Found out a lot about Zinicola and Bob.

10/2: Friday: Bob and I went to Syracuse. Went to dinner at the NCO Club with Cioci, Josephine. Went to Kenmore Hotel with Cioci. Paul came. Bob and I danced and danced. I danced with Paul too. Cioci with Bob. It was 3:30 when we left. We stayed in Dewitt, Colonial Motel because we couldn't drive back. We got home at 12:30 Sat. afternoon.

10/10: Bob and I were going to dinner but his cousin Johnny came so he called me to tell me he was going to cut trees. They must have been drinking. Bob was on his way to Utica when he got in a bad accident on Soule Road. Smashed the front end of his Starfire bad. Bent the steering wheel with his chest. Victoria called from Faxton Hospital. I went down. They took X-rays. Cut his chin with his teeth-cracked one of his ribs. Hurt his knee and I think broke his nose.

10/11: Was at Victoria's from 2:00 to 6:00 with Bob and Marc and Missy. He rested a little. He worked in spite of the accident. I went to Mrs. Penar's about Bob-she knows him well and there is something between Bob and her daughter but they are hiding it well.

10/12: Bob said the parole officer said we are not married. I had it written down that he would tell me after yesterday.

10/14: Bob and I went out. Went to the Gardens in Frankfort. Howard and Betty were there. Bob hinted to me that he knew about Monday and what I did. He knew 5 minutes after it happened, so she called him, so they are all in this thing together and Mrs. Zinicola is somewhere up north near him, I'm sure. He is really trying to give me the screws.

10/16: Went for coffee with Lou at 10:20-got back at 11:20. Kissed me.

10/17: Called Bill. Am going to see him to talk about children.

10/18: Bill called. Made an appointment for Monday at 8:00 to talk.

10/19: Bob sent me ½ dozen red roses because we had a fight over the weekend.

10/31: Went to NYC with Bob to tow a car. Got back at 2:00 p.m. Sunday.

11/19: **Bob beat me up tonight, very badly. My jaw is all black and blue and swollen. I'm-I'm finished with him. He is a very sick man-insane.**

11/20: Had X-rays at the hospital of my jaw. It's cracked. Can't move my neck either. Doctor gave me pain pills. **Told everyone I fell and hit the dresser.**

11/22: Bob rang the doorbell. Thought I wanted to see him about the tire because I went by the garage at 11 p.m. I said no, he kissed my hand and said we will be friends. He is sick.

11/25: Bob called me in the morning to wish me a Happy Thanksgiving.

11/28: Bob called at 5:30, talked 'till 5:30. He came over and stayed 'till 8:30. Refused to pay support. Called at 10:30, said a lot of what I said made sense..

12/5: Week today since I've heard from Bob.

12/6: Bill called at 7:30 a.m. am going to meet him next Wednesday nite, again to talk. I can't let him see the children now that he has two others with someone else. I have to see a priest.

12/15: Bill and I went Christmas shopping. We spent $100.00 on the kids. At 11:30 the girl, Ellen, he lives with called me and wanted to talk to him. I told her he wasn't here, he was at work, and she said ,"please let me talk to him if he's there, it's important." I told her he was at work, and he was.

12/16: Bob came at 11:00 to talk to me about what we are going to do. Put three tires on my car. He and I are supposed to go Christmas shopping Tuesday nite.

12/17: Went to the hospital Xmas party. Bev, Marion, Mirium, me. Afterwards to Twin Ponds. Uncle Hiney was suppose to meet Lou, but didn't.

12/18: Had coffee with Lou and kids at 3:00.

12/25: Bob was here in the morning. Stayed last night. Left at 10:30. Bill cam to see the children the first time in 5 years-11:30 to 3;30. We went to Julie's, the kids got so much things. Chucky called to wish a Merry Christmas. Got a Mother's ring from Bob-a cameo set from Bill.

Undated notes in the diary:

Dear Bob- went downtown-should be back by 3:30. Wait if you come.

Reverse side: Dear Andy: Waited! Love Hoss.

Honey: Good luck with your job interview. I won't be gone long. Come here as soon as you're finished because I'll be anxious to know how things turn out. I love you. Andy. (over) P.s. Don't lock the door because I have no key. Love you-Me. (over) I love you baby more than anything in the world. God bless you. Love.

Honey: The door is open. I left the couch open too. Took my Mother to the doctor. Be back later. Love you. Andy.

Ripped cardboard: Darling Andy: I love you-your honey.

Dearest darling Hoss: I have gone shopping, left at 4;45, don't know what time I'll be back. I have a picture for you. Come back today. With all my love, Andy. (Reverse side) Dearest Darling Andy: I was here at 6:05. Missed you-Love you. Give me a call around 8:30, OK? With all my love. Hoss. FINAL ENTRY IN DIARY.

The reporting and publication of personal thoughts, arrangements and desires, may be considered intrusive, by some. It is a documentary by a person who was closest to the perpetrator, otherwise identified as a "loner". The revealing parts are apparent. Although abused and forgiving, they nonetheless accepted him as a father, lover and became enablers for his continued behavior. It displays a fervent desire to reconcile differences, acceptance of his aberrant behavior and his duality. The question remains, as to the revelation that his wife knew that Ms. Zinicola had left the area earlier than the police or her family. The mystery of the vanishing family is still present.

The author could have assumed a license to remove or embellish on the interview and diary, but he did not, adjust or include, any words to enhance or romance the style of the text.

The Garrow, Hatch, Roman Coincidence

A mysterious correlation arose between Sgt. Roman, Hatch and a man named. Robert Garrow. The circumstances were reviewed by the Supreme Court of the United States and the result provoked a book written and copyrighted in 1984 called "Privileged Information." The essence of the book was whether the attorneys who represented the accused killer in a series of murders should have disclosed the location of two of the victims. The attorneys relied on the Bar Association's Oath of Admission when they swore to, "Maintain the confidentiality and preserve inviolate the secrets of my client." The sanction for disclosure and the violation of the oath can lead to disbarment.

Susan Petz, 20 years old and a student at Boston College was missing since June 1973. Alicia Hauck, a 16 year old was missing since July, 1973. In December, 1973, a Syracuse University student, Robert Morrison, saw the remains of what appeared to be a body, as he was walking through a cemetery adjacent to the campus. Ten days after the gruesome discovery, Alicia Hauck's remains were found in an airshaft near Mineville, New York, near the Canadian border. Robert Garrow was a suspect in both murders.

The mirrored images of Hatch and Garrow came to pass as Garrow took the stand during his trial. The attorneys representing him felt the only defense for their client was insanity. Garrow, as did Hatch during the kidnap and rape case in Frankfort Gorge, told his victims he was a cop or Park Police. Hatch wore a Trooper's stetson and told his victims he was a cop also.

Garrow decided to be sworn as his lawyers attempted to bolster their defense of insanity by reviewing the history of Garrow's 7 admitted rapes and four murders. Hatch also took the stand but never admitted to any murders, only attempts at an alibi at the time of the Turner murder.

The parents of Alicia and Susan pestered the defense attorneys to disclose, if they knew, where their daughters were buried. Despite knowing the locations, as Garrow had told them their whereabouts, they refused to breach their oath of privileged information, lawyer-client. .It would seem that a simple solution to a complex problem would have been for Armani and Belge to send the families a letter, unsigned and anonymous, a description of where their daughters were with a sketch or map where the bodies could be found, thus receiving some form of solace and removing the anxiety of their fate and location.

Sergeant Roman would be a guest lecturer for the various criminal justice courses. The Garrow connection was an appropriate tale to deliver to the constitutional law class. The class would finally have a person who was enmeshed in a case that was argued before the Supreme Court of the United States, standing in front of them. He began his story by relating the background of the two missing persons and the trial of Robert Garrow, the murderer. He then spoke of his chance meeting with a man from Syracuse, in a bar in New York Mills. Being a social person he struck up a conversation and his new acquaintance and was surprised at the importance of the small talk.

After determining that Roman was a State Police Sergeant and feeling some trust, he related his tale. " I got a DWI in Syracuse Sarge and you know I had one too many, flunked the breathalyzer, got bailed and worried about my license being pulled. I travel a lot and It'd mean my job. So I got these lawyers, Belge and Armani, a couple of slick guys, hoping I'd get off on a DWAI. They wanted five hundred bucks, up front and no guarantee of success. I had seventy five bucks in my checking account and was ready to take the consequences. They offered me a trade, sort of: take a picture for us and we'll wave the retainer. What they wanted me to do was to go to Oakwood Cemetery, next to the University, snap a picture of a grave and they'd wipe out their fee. They drew me a map, furnished a camera and I got free representation. I found out later it was the grave of that sixteen year old that was missing for so long. I always worried about being an accessory. My question to you, Sarge, is, did I do the right thing?"

Roman kept the discussion between a few select people. In March of 1975, Major Charland requested and received a commendation for Maynard. The casual conversation became the crux of the case as it was the exclusive proof that the attorneys knew the exact location of the missing girl's body and refused to share their knowledge with the grieving parents. The informant was subpoenaed before the Grand Jury and Belge was indicted on two counts of the Public Health Law. Roman's teaching point for the students was, law enforcement must always be assisted by luck and not always determination.

Garrow's natural life sentence ended when a failed escape in a downstate prison as an ENCON officer shot and killed him, after being abetted by Garrow's wife and son.

Pulcini's

Drawing a parallel to the title of the first chapter, The messenger, telling Hatch that his daughter had died, left an eerie feeling. Not being in the obituary should not have made him left out, none of his friends would have attended the wake or the funeral. His brother-in-law, John Pulcini and his sister, Victoria, evidently didn't get the word from Cassie's children or husband. It's improbable that an equation was made between the writer and Mr. Weaver, but the words did. The Pulcini's would blame, and they may have, the Department of Corrections, the prosecutor, judge, jury and the author.

Hatch has, what is called a MPI, (minimum period of incarceration). His earliest release date, if in fact there is not time added or bad time, would have been the minimum, 25 years. His sentencing date was April 11, 1975, his MPI would be 2000. He has met the parole board 4 times since then and has been denied. His next appearance will be 2010. Ninety days before his meetings a letter has been forwarded, by the author, to the board. A summary of the murder of Mrs. Turner, a review of the failed appeal and the knowledge that the denizens of Steuben are stricken with fear about the possibility of his release, were outlined. The letters were sent registered mail, so they were received, but never acknowledged.

On December 31, 2008, as I have in the past, a letter was sent to Hatch. The theme is always the same. Sparking his memory, mention is made that a book is being written and it would be helpful written questions would be acceptable if he decides to decline a face to face interview. At age sixty nine and having a father that died at age 47, the thought was that he may want to reveal the location of Mrs. Zinicola and her three boys. This year I included some words of sympathy for losing his daughter, Cassandra, at such an early age and added "She was a fine and dedicated mother."

Fifteen days after the mailing to Auburn Correctional Facility, P.O. Box, inmate number 75C0200, a telephone call was received. The voice was unfamiliar but recognized as a female voice. The person said, "When did Cassie die? What did she die from and where did she live?" Knowing it was prompted by the letter, a detailed acknowledgement was delivered. Asking the identity, she responded "Victoria!" A diatribe followed and listening patiently, she went on. "Why are you writing a book about my brother, to make money? He was set up by the troopers, the Utica cops told me that. We don't want you going to Auburn to question him, I'm calling the warden and tell him not to let you in. Stay out, do you hear me? You trying to make some money? Mind your own business." At that moment a male voice got on the phone and barked, "You better not go there, I'm warning you." Before an appropriate answer was spoken to include the fact that it is up to Hatch as to whether he wants to meet with me and unless I'm put on his visitors list, I'd be denied entrance, the phone went dead. They also inferred that I got his ID number through devious means as well as his address

Remaining resolute and secure in the fact that money was not a motivator, nor intention, a supposition was made: Hatch had not heard from his daughter in 16 years, nor have the Pulcini's kept in touch with her since they didn't know where she lived It wasn't a shock, as the obituary omitted his name as a survivor or included her maiden name, Hatch. Their kindred relationship is understandable but fails to be admirable. They testified under oath, called perjury and provided an alibi for a person that mutilated an innocent person for no apparent reason. Their testimony was baseless when they said, on the witness stand, that their brother, brother-in-law, was at a TV repair shop in Waterville at the time of murder. Their lies were denounced by the jury.

Hatch's mother-in-law, Cassies grandmother:

She was in her seventies, well kept, matronly and a strong personality. Helena Rooney was her name and she was the mother of Andrea, Hatch's ex wife. She was seen infrequently at his trial. We first crossed paths at a meeting of a group called, "Street Time,"

that was basically an informal group who were attempting at placing ex-offenders in jobs after their release from jail or prison. The term rehabilitation wasn't the purpose, reform was the better choice.

She was taking a couple of college courses and didn't feel uncomfortable around teenagers, in fact she seemed to enjoy it. After a meeting she approached the writer and asked if she could speak to me at length, someday, in private. She called her deceased daughter Andi and Cassandra, Cassy. We agreed on a date and time.

It seemed as if she wanted to unload on someone and I was willing to listen. She knew I had interviewed Cassy and maybe wanted to clarify some of her thoughts. She didn't object when I asked if I could take notes.

Her opening barrage was about Cassy. "She's an obsession with me, I had to drop one class because of her. I can't say no to her. She's got this guy living upstairs with her and the two kids and promising me to pay rent, which I haven't seen and he just got out of prison. I always seem to be surrounded by bad people." She transitioned to Cassy's father quickly and without a question, probably because her granddaughter had spoken to her about the odd behavior between Hatch and his mother.

"One time we went to South Carolina, Parris Island, Bob was in the Marines, his mother, Vickie, Andie and me. Boy did his mother stick to him, Andie and me in the back, Vicky wanted to sit next to him and there was a big fight so he agreed to hold his mother's hand

and drive with the other. This went on for hundreds of miles. I think Vicky and his mother were jealous of each other. Do you think that's strange?" The question was rhetorical.

She shifted to Andrea. "When Andie had Cassy, she was 20, they called her a scientific baby, born with a halo, sorry, a veil. When she was born she had no blood on her and when I asked, who cleaned her up, the nurse said, 'she was born that way.' The astrologers say that anyone born with a veil will be brilliant. I wish she'd come back to college." She launched into history as she said, "Andrea's real name is Hillary, born on St. Hillary's Day. We were all named after saints, Cassy's middle name is the same as mine, Helena."

Without prompting, she went on, "Let me tell you something else that's peculiar. Cassy was baptized with two other baby boys, both named Bernard, and guess what else, Linda and Lisa Cady were buried from St. Bernard's Church in Waterville. How do you like that." She also said there was a name connection between Victoria naming her daughter Lisa Ann but didn't connect it with the Cady's.

Returning to Cassy she said, "You know she took this car when she was 13, drove to Stockbridge, picked up her half brother and half sister and drove to Syracuse. My sister called me and brought them home. No big deal for me but Bill Smith, the kids dad, thought it was."

Venturing into Cassy's life, the question was, "How about her last count, possession of stolen property?" She replied, "Oh that, cost me $3,000 for the lawyer. I had sold my mother's house on Williams Street for $7,000 and its all gone. I told you I was compulsive about her, I can't say no." Her next statement was incomprehensible when she said, "There's some new history coming up, just listen. Pisces are unpredictable, they have a strong feeling for human beings, they have their own religion, that's Cassy."

"Cassy said you asked about Bob's relationship with that Zinicola. She was a Penar, she used to live near my cousin on Sunset Ave. Her mother is dead, killed on the Arterial. Now wasn't that something? No, I don't know her." A follow up was, "Do you feel he killed her and the boys?" The reply was qualified, "That's the question."

"Cassy said her father calls you often, tell me about the conversations." "Yeah, he calls me about 2 or 3 times a month, collect of course. I had a bill of $450.00 one month, got an unlisted number but now I'm listed. I'm what you might call a 'Brave coward.' When he calls he asks about Cassy, we sometimes talk for 45 minutes. I don't think about him being in prison, I think he's down the street. I don't ask about him, how he is, how he feels, what he does. Should I?"

A decision was made to broach the murder of Mrs. Turner. "What's your take on Hatch killing Mary Rose Turner, Mrs. .Rooney?" I was stunned by the answer. "Did he?" she bolted. My patience was being tested when I said, "C'mon Mrs. Rooney, the jury said he did."

"You know how much he weighs? Cassy took a picture of him, she says he weighs 300 pounds and has a waist like yours, 30-32 maybe."

Choosing another slant, I asked, "Does he blink, Mrs. Rooney?" She didn't seem to be surprised at the question and without pondering she said, "He blows his nose all the time, he was always reaching for his hanky. Did you know you don't have to blink if you clear your head, your sinuses, of liquid that goes to your eyes-see- if you blow your nose a lot you don't have to blink.".

When asked how she reacted to Cassy having a tattoo on her left arm she reached forward in disbelief and said, "She has no such thing." She quickly changed the subject and said, "Did you know that if you are born before noon time, no one rules you ?" I had never heard that and didn't care to be aware of it.

Helena volunteered her aggressiveness toward the man who had abused her daughter and may have precipitated her suicide when she said, "You may know that I hit him 3 or 4 times, right across his face. When he asked why, I said, 'I wanted to know how I'd feel.' He said, 'Go ahead' and I did. So there. I felt good, I was in control and not afraid."

The interview started to wind down. Her parting comment was, "You know, I'd be rich today if I wasn't afraid of cats, dogs and the dark. My husband and me always slept with a light on overhead, all night long."

With few, if any conclusive analysis, it would best left to a person with the training, such as Dr. Bigelow.

Indifference

The Hatch family had a contemptuous attitude towards the State Police, saying they had targeted him soon after the homicide. The accusation wasn't accurate. Following the finding of Mrs. Turner's decimated body there was a vast but concentrated sifting through people of interest. The scores of interviews, the documentation and reports covered 323 entries over three months. Every lead was followed and nothing was neglected as they pursued evidence. Every caller was questioned and received the dignity of a follow up. The extensive list had as an inclusion, "No further information obtained."

The State Police are trained in the techniques of questioning and an interview is always ended by the query," Is there anyone you know who could contribute or add to your information that would be helpful to us?" Often unsupported conclusions such as gossip, small talk, can be attested to by the question.

Interviews are logged, indexed and reviewed by a superior, the lead investigator, who may request a call back to the subject. Hatch became only one of hundreds of suspects, not the sole convicted felon in the area and certainly the troopers didn't think he had a bulls-eye on his back. Admittedly he had his trailer under surveillance, as all prime witnesses should be. His M.O., prior criminal history, proximity to where Mrs. Turner was last seen and his vehicle matching the observers descriptions, placed him high on the scale of probabilities.

To illustrate Hatch's icy, sang froid personality, a paragraph is worthy of repeating a scene. After the warrant was served, hours before his parole release date, he was cuffed and transported to the Oneida County jail in Oriskany. After processing and sanitizing, the escorting trooper returned to his squad car. Remembering he had left his clip board outside the holding cell with the booking papers, he returned to the jail, gained entrance and walked to Hatch's holding cell. The trooper said it was less than 3 minutes from the time he last saw him until he returned. He was astounded when he eyed the man, who was facing 25 to life, lying on his back, snoring. He expressed it as a horrible, eerie feeling. It became another observation of a deviant person. It was in this jail that he would have a conversation with Joseph Nowak the following April that would help to seal his fate at the time of his trial.

Assigned personnel and assisting agencies

In an effort to include all of the individuals who participated in the investigation and whose names may not be cited in the index, it seemed important to embody those who were assigned a role.

State Police Uniformed:
Major R.S. Charland
Captains: G.M. Chromey, G.A. Loomis
Lieutenant M.J. Mullins
F/Sgt. F.A. Fesenger
Z/Sgts: M.T. Roman, T.N. Kruk
Sgts: R.B. Gallo, P.B. Rocker, R.C. Julian, B.J. Stack
T/Sgts: Preston, Warjas, Sackel
Troopers: M.J. Jasek, R.S. Suffolk, D.T. Wallace, H.J. Menges, R. Novier, G.L. Wendt, T.A. Klara, J.V. Parker, D.A. Link, T.R. Kelly, G.T. Darby, A.J. Smith, A.S. Jess, R.E. Malecki, R.W. Swayze, D.L. Bergstrom, A.L. Lonsberry, L.J. Moylan, M.G. Michelson, H.E. Allen, D.J. Cesari, C.H. Deans, F.J. Euron, R.A. Boxall, W.T. Loveric, D.A. Geary, I.K. Parkhurst, W.F. Chesebro, J.E. Chaffee, P.D. LaGatta, A.C. Bitely, A.L. Broccoli, J.M. PaladinoG.E. Hopper, R.W. Reese, W.T. Fitzgerald, M.T. Sullivan, T.C. Romando, R.A. Sypec, R.F. Sfeir, D.H. Cole, J.N. Wayland-Smith, E.F. Lawson, F.E. Bockardt, K.C. McConnell,

State Police B.C.I:
Capt. C. G. Griffin
Lt. G.E. Brown
Sr. Investigators: T.F. Gallagher, D.V. Pearson, R.J. Gildersleeve, McKinley, F. Peo, Conley, J. Arcuri.
Investigators: T.F. Ash, C. Donovan, T.J. Carl, G.P. Thomas, D.F. Traub, D.J. Arcuri, N.A. Cerro, J.T. Oczkowski, L. Bartkowiak, M.P. Cryan, D.B. Wassal, M.J. Restatnte, J.T. Doyle, G.J. Corbett, E.S. Friedman, R.F. Hojnacki, J.H. Briant, E.P. Fitzpatrick.

Utica Police Department:
Chief B. Rotundo
Deputy Chief, N. Yaghy

Captain M. Taurisano
Lt. R. Pecheone
C.I.D. investigators, Uniformed patrolmen.

U.S. Treasury Department:
Special Agent Richard Weller, ATF

N.Y. State Conservation Dept.
Game protectors and Forest Rangers:
Thomas Oatman, Fred Feisthemel, Oscar Hammer, William Barker, Eric Mynter, Henry Madison, William Graves, Donald Buehler

Army National Guard, 104th M.P. Battalion
Colonel R. Clayton, Commander
Major R. Evans, Bn. Commander

The jury
Terrence E. Kehoe, Foreman, New Harford
Louisa Madden, Sherrill
Mary T. Servatius, Utica
Betty Deely, Blossvale
Henry C. Spellicy, Camden
James B. Heilig, Rome
Jack L. Delaney, North Bay
Ken G. Halliday, Oriskany
Orlando G. Halliday, Oriskany
George Motto, New Hartford
Joseph Vendetti, Utica
Arthur C. Woodruff, Rome
Willis H. Carr, New Hartford
Wesley Vanderhorst, Clinton
Tom R. Polarolo, Utica
David Farnsworth, Camden

His relentless pursuit of the Hatch case was not an odyssey but a quest for the truth, justice and a term he lived by-----"Just Desserts." There were terms used by his trooper brethren describing his relentless fixation with the conviction of Hatch by saying he was obsessed. He probably fitted that description. Twenty five to life wasn't enough for him to be satisfied, he felt that it was just the border of the puzzle. He wanted to crack the Cady and Zinicola cases.

When he'd discuss the Cady and Zinicola murders and disappearance, he'd allude to the sequence of the slayings by uttering, emotionally, "Linda and Lisa Cady. They couldn't be murdered at the same time, one died first, the other watched while either the mother saw her child die or the child saw her mother die. Now the Zinicola's, three boys and their mom, who died first and who saw the other three slaughtered? Think about it. I'll get that no good bastard or I'll die trying." He has since died and he did try.

Psychiatric Profile
The two page report was signed, "Newton Bigelow, M.D. Attending Psychiatrist, Marcy State Hospital." He was unduly modest as his title should have included that he was considered one of the most respected and stellar psychiatrist in the State of New York. Among his many titles included the Director of Mental Health, State of New York, appointed under the governorship of Averill Harriman. He could have modestly signed the report as Director, Marcy Psychiatric Hospital. Ostentatious was never used in describing him.

Eight days after the dismembered body of Mrs. Turner was excavated from her grave, Captain Griffin of the NYSP asked for his intervention: a profile of who would perform such a merciless crime. His report was accurate and descriptive and it pointed to their suspect, Bernard Paul Hatch.

He began by reviewing the details, of the degrading ritual, cunning actions of covering up his tracks by mutilation and aggressive tendencies directed at older women. He spoke to the Parole Board members who shared with him the history of Hatch to include the fact that he was breast fed until he was five years old and his mother was observed kissing him with more than maternal affection. His aberrant behavior was atypical as he recited that he was a loner, over meticulous and had a disregard for law and inability to learn from experience.

The report from the profiler included some descriptions and Hatch's predilections such as resistance to the sexual act. An interview with his daughter validated this compulsion. Hatch, for some weird reason, told his daughter that when he and his wife went on their honeymoon, he put a pistol to her head and became orgasmic as she screamed in horror.

Acknowledgments

My sincere and deep appreciation is extended to my friend, Frank J. Macner, Major USAF Retired, who was instrumental in many ways as this book was completed. Without his encouragement and abilities, the words would have remained in limbo and never evolve into reality.

I am thankful for the help my eldest daughter Kyle, J.D., and her husband, Dr. Peter Ladd gave me and for their generous time and proficiency, while editing the manuscript.

To M.L. Dilworth, who performed numerous tasks and spent countless hours while collating and coordinating the myriad of reports and transcripts available.

It is vital that accolades and gratitude be mentioned and directed to the many students from the Criminal Justice Department who accepted the task of hunting and scouring the Steuben countryside for evidence and graves. Their time and effort was voluntary and helpful and my thoughts are shared by the New York State Police

For their encouragement and concern for justice, my thanks are offered to the multitude of students that I meet since retirement, as they ask, "Have you finished the Hatch book yet?" It was their prodding and prompting that urged me to complete my task and quest.

And to my wife, Mary Jane, who shared her skills as an elementary teacher as she assisted me in my limited journalism ability, aiding me in the basics: grammar, syntax, content and spelling. Her many years of patience during this rocky road, as I pursued my goal, she was unstinting in her allegiance.

The only remorse I possess, upon finalizing the book, is what I didn't say to my original collaborators. I wish I had been forthcoming and expressed my admiration and esteem for them. Although the book bears my name as the author, it rightfully belongs to my departed friends and true masters, Ted, Maynard and Gil.

About The Author

Thomas Blanchfield holds a B.S. from Niagara University, a M.A. from the State University of New York and a graduate of Command and General Staff College, Fort Leavenworth and the Army War College, Carlisle PA He holds a Professor Emeritus, Criminal Justice title from Mohawk Valley College, Utica, N.Y. Following retirement he was an Adjunct Professor at Utica College and SUNY.

He was a licensed Private Investigator and a Commissioner on the Oneida County Conditional Release Commission from 1987 to 1993. He was the training director of the basic and supervisors academy at the New York State Police Academy in Albany from 1987 to 1993. He shares his time between Clinton, N.Y. and Hutchinson Island, Florida

Index

Buffalo, N.Y., 20
Bush, R., 89
Byrnes, Clyde, 54
Byrnes, William, 46-50, 54, 56

Cable, Robert, 24, 69, 78, 81, 99
Cady, Linda, 50, 79, 89-91, 97-100, 102, 108, 111, 113, 114, 120, 135
Cady, Lisa Ann, 50, 89-91, 97,-100, 102, 108, 111, 113, 114, 120, 135
Cape Vincent, 127
Carl, T.J, 45, 46, 48-50, 59, 60, 68, 80, 82, 89, 94, 117
Cassandra (nee Hatch), 63-65, 1, 195, 106, 108, 109, 111, 114, 125, 132-136
Cavoli, Brian, 16
Central Motel, 45, 49
Cerro, N.A., 50
Chaffee, J.E. 14-17, 37-39, 43, 51, 70, 74, 77, 100, 111
Chapple, Christine, 80
Chapple, Joseph, 90, 99
Charland, R.S. 43-45, 48, 51, 68, 87, 93, 94, 132
Chesebro, W.F., 63, 64
Chromey, G.M., 37
Cioci, 127
Clinton, 25
Colgate University, 104, 105
Command Post, 42, 45, 50, 51
Corelli, Anthony, 24, 25, 69, 78
Cornhill Savings and Loan, 91, 114
Court Street, 23, 24, 45, 49, 78, 90
Criminal Justice Program, 106
Culver Ave., 36

Dannemora, 117
Darmer, Jeffrey, 117
Darrigrand, Arthur, 59-61, 65
Deansboro, 65, 90, 122
"Debbie" (alias), 95
D.N.A. 73, 103
D.O.C.S., 95
Dodge, Nelson, 20
Dwyer, Viola, 21, 22